Praise for *A New Way Forward for Schools*

'This is an extraordinary gift of a book on every level: its content and design reduce overwhelm; it relies on us to create from a clear sense of calling; it encourages, supports and guides us educators into promising possibilities. And it respects and honours us for who we have chosen to be.'
– Dr Margaret Wheatley, author of 13 books, from *Leadership and the New Science* (1992) to *Restoring Sanity: Practices to Awaken Generosity, Creativity, and Kindness* (2024)

'In an age of incessant distractions, here is a book that refocuses our collective mission – teaching and learning. The Unleash Learning System provides a research-based guide to improving student learning. It provides a shared language to support leaders to keep their teachers and schools working on what is most important – students.'
– Mary Chiodo, Campus Principal, Copperfield College

'Steeped in evidence and rich with practical strategies, *A New Way Forward for Schools* is an essential resource for school leaders seeking to streamline practices into sustainable systems. Dr William DeJean provides a thoughtful and actionable approach to reducing cognitive overload for both teachers and leaders, offering a clear pathway to more effective and efficient schools. This book is both empowering and deeply attuned to the challenges leaders face in the modern era.'
– Karen Corbett, secondary school leader, Western Australia

'This book shows us the way to keep our focus on what's important – student learning. This system will not only reduce teacher and leader overwhelm, but it will also vastly improve learning for all students. It brings together one whole system we can introduce into our schools that keeps us focused on the main game.'
– Genevieve Simson, former school principal

'This book isn't just one more thing. **It is the thing!** It clearly shows how to pull instruction together into an elegant meaningful system that makes sense to rather than confuses teachers and administrators and students themselves.'
– Professor Emerita Jacqueline Thousand, California State University, San Marcos

'This is a "must read" for those in educational leadership seeking to implement effective approaches to enhancing long-term learning for all students. If you are seeking to maximise the learning potential in your school, this book is for you.'
– Dr Sally Knipe, former Associate Professor Education, Charles Darwin University

A New Way *Forward* for Schools

Dr William DeJean

A New Way *Forward* for Schools

Advancing Teaching and Learning in the Era of Overwhelm

Published in 2025 by Amba Press, Melbourne, Australia
www.ambapress.com.au

© William DeJean 2025

All rights reserved. No part of this book may be reproduced or transmitted in any form or by any means, electronic or mechanical, including photocopying, recording or by any information storage and retrieval system, without prior permission in writing from the publisher.

Cover design: Tess McCabe
Internal design: Amba Press
Editor: Andrew Campbell

ISBN: 9781923215702 (pbk)
ISBN: 9781923215719 (ebk)

A catalogue record for this book is available from the National Library of Australia.

To Dr Nancy Farnan.
You helped light a flame 30 years ago
and continue to help it shine brightly.

Acknowledgments

Love, as defined by bell hooks, is a consistent message of love and kindness (Hooks, 2001). Fortunately for me, my life is surrounded by people whose actions mirror this definition and have also helped unleash this book's potential. The fun part for me is that I get to acknowledge some of them here.

To my partner, Robert Thorniley, who can flesh out the argument of any piece of text like no one I know! And whose wisdom, kindness, love and encouragement fill my life and this book.

To Karen Corbett, Mary Chiodo-Jennings, Genevieve Simson and Dr Jacque Thousand for reading the manuscript, sharing the conversations and leading the way. You continue to be great examples and wonderful teachers for me.

To David, who has shared 'stories of success' with me when 'success' felt very far away. Thank you for your support, insight, knowledge and the many coffees by the harbour.

To Dr Nina Potter for your data expertise, enthusiasm and deep kindness. Thank you!

And to all the leaders, educators and schools who have put these ideas into practice. Thank you for making me aware of the positive impact and for the many ways you use this work to make things better for our world.

Onwards!

Contents

Introduction 1

Part 1: The Era of Overwhelm 7

Chapter 1   Can't Keep Up? This Might Be Why 9
Chapter 2   Leading Learning in the Era of Overwhelm ... 27

Part 2: Systems Thinking in the Era of Overwhelm ... 35

Chapter 3   Embedding a Shared Teaching and Learning Mission ... 37
Chapter 4   What Makes Learning Stick for Everyone 45
Chapter 5   The System That Makes Learning Stick for Everyone ... 59

Part 3: Advancing Teaching and Learning in the Era of Overwhelm ... 99

Chapter 6   Using a Staged Approach 101
Chapter 7   Leading the Efforts 113
Chapter 8   Implementation and the Use of Data 121

Conclusion: Creating Impact That Endures 133
About the Author 141
Next Steps 143
References 145

Introduction

If you've picked up this book, you and possibly your team are wanting to (or working to) advance teaching and learning across your school.

You might be a principal, a district/network leader, a superintendent, an assistant principal, part of the executive team, a KLA or department chair, an instructional coach, a mentor of new teachers or someone who is focusing on advancing teaching and learning across the school.

If you're reading these words, I'm guessing you're committed to the work you're doing and believe that effective teaching and learning can be a force for good for students and our world. You want to advance teaching and learning across your school because you know your school has the potential to go to the next level of success. You and your team want to expand your school's impact. For good.

By advancing teaching and learning schoolwide, I'm guessing what you want is to:

- move good teaching to great teaching (or if it's great, move it to an advanced level) – across your school
- ensure teaching and learning are your school's number-one priority
- create a common language around high-quality teaching and learning, rather than just focusing on a variety of unconnected teaching strategies

- ensure long-term learning is sticking for all students, rather than focusing on task completion
- support teachers across your school in optimising what they do
- help your school be an innovative place for teaching and learning rather than a place of compliance.

But you might be feeling overwhelmed and stressed due to:

- constantly trying to 'keep up' with the latest new thing
- seeing teaching and learning sometimes taking a back seat to everything else your school is required to do
- feeling like you're working harder but are not sure if you're getting lasting outcomes
- getting conflicting advice around the best way to advance teaching and learning
- sometimes being buried in compliance measures that simply add to your team's overwhelm.

If you can relate to any of these aims and feelings, this book is for you.

Even if you're highly committed to advancing teaching and learning across your school, have a love of learning or are part of a team reading this book, you might not read it from cover to cover. Instead, you might scan it or search for video clips or a podcast discussion about it. The reason why has little to do with you, your commitment to our profession or your professionalism. Rather, it has to do with the new era we're now in. That era is impacting your and your team's time for thinking, learning and reflecting.

The current era might also be impacting your ability to advance teaching and learning across your school. It's safe to assume that because you're reading this book, teaching and learning are a high priority for you. Therefore, I invite you to take another step with me.

Why this book now

This book's mission is to help you understand the new era we're now in, which I call the era of overwhelm, and learn what it takes to advance teaching and learning across your school in this era. This is important because in the era of overwhelm, education has become increasingly complicated, and you and your team may find yourselves working harder and questioning if you're focusing on the right things or wondering if your leadership efforts are making a lasting impact.

The good news is that what you're about to learn won't require you to 'reinvent the wheel' or throw everything out and start over. Rather, it's designed to help you cut through the noise by showing you the structures, system and actions that can bring things together, rather than add more. The results? You'll lower stress and overload, achieve schoolwide alignment, and ensure long-term learning for every student so that what they need to know becomes theirs, for good.

Before we explore it, let me first introduce myself.

My story

I'm Dr William DeJean, founder and CEO of Unleash Learning. I'm also the host of Unleash Learning TV and Radio.

I've been deep in the education and learning field for 25 years. I have a doctorate in education and have written various articles and books on the subject that reflect what I have learned and experienced over the years.

I began my career as a high school teacher in San Diego and taught for 10 years across the US, winning the 2003 San Diego County Teacher of the Year Award.

While still teaching, I studied for a master's and doctorate in education. It was invaluable to put my theories immediately into practice and gain a broader, more inclusive understanding of how we humans learn.

I then taught at universities in the US and Australia. I worked with pre-service teachers and taught teachers as they studied for their master's degrees. I developed university courses and consulted extensively with school leadership teams. This gave me an international perspective on education, organisational change and learning that made a lasting impact.

I've also noticed something taking place wherever I go. I've finally come to understand we're now in a new era. And the era requires a new way forward.

My mission is to support innovative schools with a new way forward so leaders and teaching teams can make long-term learning stick for everyone.

I hope this book does that for you.

How to use this book

My experience tells me that if learning sticks for you, you'll be equipped to pass this on to others. That's why this book is designed to support making learning stick for you, thereby modelling fundamental concepts that are central to Unleash Learning. This book is designed for you as an instructional leader, and I recommend that you read and discuss it with others whose objectives include creating learning environments that benefit all students.

To model these processes and concepts, throughout the book you'll see actions I hope you'll take. Namely, you'll be asked to write, speak, draw, summarise or take other actions that will cause learning to stick for you.

You'll see this icon as a signal to act. In the era of overwhelm we're now in (more on this later), you might want to jump over these actions. But I hope you'll give yourself the time to intentionally engage with them.

Before we get started, there are a few agreements I invite you to make. I've found that these agreements can proactively help you make the most of this book and aid in the ways learning sticks for you.

Agreement #1:
Maintain a positivity bias

Positive psychologists tell us that we are programmed with a 'negativity bias'. That is, our brains are hardwired to look for the negative. This bias probably helped us survive. But today, it doesn't always serve us well.

It's possible that as you're reading this book your hard-wired negativity bias will emerge. It might say things to you like 'I already know this' or 'We do this' or 'This won't work for us'. Or some other negativity bias thought might emerge.

That's why I'm going to invite you to agree to maintain a positivity bias. You can do this when a negativity bias emerges, by simply asking a question like: 'How can I make this work for me?' or 'How can I make this work for our school?' If you keep that positivity bias on hand, you'll be primed to get the most out of this book.

Agreement #2:
Befriend your shadow beliefs

You come to this book already with a vast array of knowledge and expertise. This book is here to help you optimise your strengths and impact. But there's a chance that while reading it, your shadow beliefs might appear. Shadow beliefs are the parts of ourselves that we reject because we think they're unacceptable and might cause shame or a negative reaction from others (Ford, 1999). We all have them.

I've experienced for myself and seen it with people whom I've mentored that when stress, overwhelm, uncertainty or times of change occur, our shadow beliefs rise to the surface.

As you read this book, shadow beliefs such as 'I'm a bad leader. I'm a fraud. People will find out I don't know what I'm doing' or something else you're probably familiar with might emerge.

If a shadow belief emerges, rather than run away from it, I invite you to observe it and even try to befriend it. It might just need your care and attention and even help you see that you're more capable than you ever realised. Please remind yourself that it's just a shadow belief. If it arises, you might even tell it 'Oh hello there! Nice to see you again.' Or ask it: 'What do you need from me?'

And continue reading the book.

 ### Agreement #3: Trust the process

I've seen that learning doesn't always stick in real time. In the case of this book, it's possible that learning might not stick for you until the end of the book, when your team discusses it, or months after you've read it. Sticky, long-term learning often isn't a step-by-step event. Rather, it's a journey that emerges in timeframes different from our own agenda.

That's why before you begin the book, and throughout reading it, I invite you to agree to trust the process of it. And stay open to what might emerge.

Okay, if you're ready, so am I. I invite you to keep an open mind (and yes, heart, too). What you're about to read isn't a list of strategies to follow or another formula that will come and go. It's an approach that can lower your team's mental load and boost your entire school's impact.

Let's do this!

Part 1
The Era of Overwhelm

Overwhelm:

Verb. To bury or drown beneath a mass of earth, water, etc, to submerge completely; to destroy or obliterate by covering with something.

Noun. The action of overwhelming; the fact or state of being overwhelmed.

Oxford English Dictionary

Chapter 1

Can't Keep Up? This Might Be Why

Are you experiencing this?

When you look around your school, you're not in crisis and likely know that good work is taking place, but you believe it can go to the next level of success. Your school already has teaching strategies that teachers know about or use and an established curriculum. Even if your school is getting positive data results (however measured), you can see that your school is ripe for advancement. In fact, you don't want the kind of teaching and learning that's just focused on students getting through exams or completing assignments. Instead, you want the kind of teaching and learning that helps students across your entire school go on to live bigger and better lives. You believe this is possible for your school.

You might be seeing or experiencing one or more of the following across your Kindergarten to Year 12 (K–12) school (or network of schools):

- pockets of teaching and learning excellence that you don't want to interrupt

- some students being 'spoon-fed' by teachers who do most of the talking or classroom instruction
- some teachers who are doing the best they can but need more support on ways to strengthen high-quality teaching and learning
- individuals assigned to help advance teaching and learning (instructional coaches, mentors, teaching and learning champions, etc), but it is uncertain if that work is elevating the entire school
- some classrooms where the focus of instruction is only on tasks, assignments or exam completion
- students spending a large portion of instructional time in Google classroom or other online platforms to complete work
- behaviour management challenges due to passivity in the classroom.

If any of these are a yes for you, I'm guessing you know you can take things to the next level. But if figuring out the best way forward or the best way to sustain your efforts feels more difficult these days, it's not your imagination. It's because we're now in a new era. I call it **the era of overwhelm**.

In the era of overwhelm more and more is being asked of you and your school. You're buried in information, new ideas and new ways of doing things. You might find yourself trying to 'keep up' with the latest strategies, initiatives, frameworks and requirements. This environment can increase your stress and mental load as you try to keep up and, because of all the constant changes and shifts of direction, leave you questioning whether you and your team are truly creating an impact that lasts. There may be a temptation to think that if the team works hard enough or finds a way to cut the 'right things' back, it can stay on top of things, hoping that the time of overload will eventually pass.

But from my vantage point, this era is here to stay, and it's probably going to get worse. There are many reasons why. Here are just a few.

1. Technology is speeding things up

You're moving faster than ever before. To keep up, you try taking calls during your commute, answering emails during breaks and staying focused when interruptions occur, as they do all the time. Being busy and trying to keep up become the norm. And it may be difficult to believe how quickly life is passing by.

You try to hold the waters back by telling your team they don't need to check emails after hours. But the emails keep flooding in. You decide to limit the number of meetings, but when your team does meet, the agenda has just grown. You and your team might find that your time is spent just 'keeping up', causing your collective long-term thinking and planning to fall farther behind.

Because things are moving faster and people are short on time, workshops that are quick, webinars that are short, and videos that are condensed become the norm. As things move faster, it's possible there's less time for thinking and reflecting, and short-term approaches replace long-term planning. Distraction becomes the new normal.

> **Questions to consider:**
>
> How quickly do you pick up your phone? How often do staff take their phones out during meetings? How much thinking time is afforded for your team and school? How fast do things seem to be moving for you personally and professionally? How about for your school?

2. More information is being 'delivered' than ever before

When I worked on my doctoral dissertation, I had to drive to the university, park my car, walk to the library and be there for hours. (I know I look 24, but I'm a bit older! 😊) At the library I'd stand at the copy machine printing the articles I located, then often stay at the library to read them. On my walk back to my car, I'd sometimes bump into one of my professors, and we'd talk about what I had read or what I was thinking about. While there are advantages to being able to access much of this from my home, I miss the time and space I had for uninterrupted reading, thinking, discussing and questioning.

Today, information is 'delivered' to us from everywhere. The university library is a click away. Podcasts, YouTube clips, social media posts and website blogs fill up our devices. eBooks offer more to read and online platforms provide more and more to watch.

When it comes to learning, at a click of your fingers you can access courses on any subject imaginable. Micro-credentials are the new norm. In the era of overwhelm, if educators are the ones choosing a course, they might 'pick' the one that takes the least time to complete since they already have so much on their plates. In fact, your school may have so many online courses available that it's hard to know where to start!

We're being flooded with information like never before and ways and tools to 'consume' that information.

3. 'Best practices' in teaching and learning are everywhere

Each day seems to bring a new book, formula, strategy or other thing regarding what are deemed 'best practices' in teaching and learning (Heck, I've written two books on the subject).

There are great practices and important educational research to inform us. But in this era of overwhelm, without a purpose for their use or an organising structure for this information, the 'best practices' sometimes don't break through the noise or, worse, just add to the mental noise already there.

And the flood of information coming to your school can leave some people feeling inadequate because they aren't using all the 'best practices'.

Questions to consider:

What are the 'best practices' you follow? Are there educational experts or organisations you tend to rely on? How consistent is the messaging? How often do you feel like you're missing out on the latest new thing or as if your school might be left behind on what's current or, according to someone, a 'must use'?

In the space below, please record the 'best practices' you know about.

1.	2.
3.	4.
5.	6.
7.	8.

4. We are all experiencing uncertainty, disruption and change

We're an interconnected, global community. What happens on one side of the planet is quickly known about and often felt throughout the globe. An election, war, new technology, financial change, a virus, decisions made about the climate crisis or more on one side of the planet can quickly impact us all. At the very least, these happenings can provide a threat, a worry or the possibility of more change ahead. Even if you or your school are not feeling the effects, I'm guessing you're aware of what's taking place.

Plus, technology brings this information to your team, your students and their families in an instant. This environment can add to the mental and emotional overwhelm your school might be feeling – even if you don't always hear people talking about it. This includes your leadership and teaching cohorts, students, families and the community you serve.

What overwhelm can do to your school

You might be thinking: this time will pass, a new normal will set in or, if we work hard enough, we will figure this out. I'm not trying to be negative (good things are coming – please keep reading!), but the era of overwhelm is here to stay.

And it's probably going to get worse.

Without your skilled leadership and your team moving together in the same direction, this era will impact your school in numerous ways. Here are some that I've noticed, and you likely can add many more to this list.

Teaching and learning slip to the bottom of the to-do list

'We really need to focus on teaching and learning.' It's a statement I started hearing from leaders a few years ago.

When leaders would say this, I'd ask them what it meant. They'd often tell me the list of items their school had been working on: positive behaviour management initiatives, mental health training, new building construction, updated school culture processes, compliance measures and more.

It didn't mean teaching and learning weren't happening at the school.

But it indicated they wanted to ensure their leadership was helping to lead high-quality teaching and learning across the school – and that discussions, time and resources were ensuring it was a top focus. Or they were looking to find an embedded approach that would create common understanding or a shared alignment.

This wasn't an indictment of the school or the leadership team; it's a result of the era of overwhelm.

Increased mental load

Any resistance you might notice to advancing teaching and learning across your school might not mean that your team isn't supportive or committed to teaching and learning excellence. It might come from people believing this new initiative will be just one more fad, or they're simply protecting their cognitive load.

A cognitive load is the amount of information that fills a person's brain (Plass et al., 2010). My experience suggests, in this new era, that many people are living with overload.

It's important to remember this because there's a new way forward that we're going to explore that can lower your team's cognitive load while boosting their teaching and learning impact.

Fear

Positive emotions prime people for learning (Green, 2014) and can cause people to broaden their viewpoint and build personal resources (Fredrickson, 2009). If you experience positive emotions, you might also notice that you feel more creative, make connections, look for similarities rather than differences or see a bigger picture. It's also a reason why I invited you to have a positivity bias at the start of this book!

Fear can cause the opposite to happen. It can cause us to narrow our focus, retreat, pull back, protect or lose sight of a bigger picture. Fear can sap passion (Pressfield, 2014) or, in the worst case, close out options for innovation and positive change.

Shadow beliefs emerge

Your teaching and leadership team come with a vast array of skills, knowledge and talents, but when people are under stress, don't feel grounded or feel overwhelmed (the new normal, I say), shadow beliefs can emerge.

As I mentioned in the introduction, shadow beliefs are the parts of ourselves that we reject because we think they're unacceptable or might cause shame or a negative reaction from others.

Below you'll find some of the shadow beliefs I've had, been told about or overheard.

 **To feel the impact of these shadow beliefs, please read them out loud.**

- I'm a bad leader.
- I'm a bad teacher.
- I'm not good at this.
- I'm incompetent.
- I'm a fraud.
- Other people have this figured out.
- I don't know what I'm doing.

Shadow beliefs, when examined, integrated or brought into the light, can turn into great gifts. (That's for another book. We've got important work to do here!) But in this era, it's important to know about your own shadow beliefs and be aware that some of your team will probably have them too.

This is especially important to be aware of as you're getting ready to advance teaching and learning across your school, because shadow beliefs can emerge during different parts of that journey.

Questioning meaning and purpose

You and your team probably entered our profession based on strongly held values and beliefs. You do the work you do because you're working toward a specific outcome that connects to your personal why (Palmer, 1998). In fact, science suggests that high levels of meaning and purpose connect to wellbeing (Seligman, 2011; Falecki, 2023). But in the era of overwhelm, people can work very hard but be left questioning if they're really making a difference or wondering if the latest initiative is worth their effort and time, especially if it's seen as one more thing that will come and go.

This can also lead to what scientists refer to as cognitive dissonance. That is when someone holds contradictory thinking – in this case, understanding that change is needed but being unsure if the change is worth the effort.

Later, we'll talk about ways your leadership can help support your team in staying connected to their meaning and purpose, or if you're already working on this, additional ways you might consider.

Lack of alignment

Your new teachers are taking induction programs. Some of your experienced teachers have attended a conference about supporting students with mental health. Your leadership team learn about a new literacy framework the state will require to be 'delivered' throughout your school.

At times you ask individuals to present what they've learned during staff meetings or professional learning days, hoping that the information will spread and impact practice.

Your team observes areas that would support your school's success, so you bring in guest speakers to run professional learning sessions but come to wonder if this information is causing more feelings of overwhelm and only short-term gains.

Some of the people you've invested in leave for another school. Your best instructional coach decides to retire. You're working hard but struggle to create full alignment among your leadership team, new and experienced teachers, instructional coaches, mentors and more. Or if you have a teaching and learning framework, you wonder if that framework is advancing teaching and learning or is just another document of compliance that sits on a shelf.

More pressure on schools

In the era of overwhelm, increasing pressure can be placed on schools to 'get it right' by parents, politicians and other stakeholders who are demanding certainty and stability and the right kind of impact.

Technology is quickly changing what jobs are available, while living expenses increase and things that once seemed in reach for many might feel like they're only for a few. Getting it right means ensuring students have the right skill sets, learn the right things (which might keep changing), and are prepared for the right jobs so they can participate in a global economy that can change seemingly overnight.

If you're wanting to advance teaching and learning across your school, this pressure adds to your decision making. It can leave you wondering what the best things are to focus on that will cause a lasting impact.

Leaders struggle to advance teaching and learning in the era of overwhelm

You've made the commitment to advance teaching and learning across your school but there are choices to now make to decide which is the best way forward. You've conducted classroom observations, have data (you're probably inundated and overwhelmed by it) and might even have mandates from the district or state. But if making the decision on what's the best way forward feels challenging, there's nothing wrong with you. It's the era of overwhelm! Here are a few things that might be adding to the struggle.

1. Being busy with other things

A school is a teaching and learning organisation. That might seem obvious, but in the era of overwhelm more and more is often asked of a school. Wellbeing programs, sporting events, maintaining connection with your feeder schools, excursions, mentoring initiatives, positive behaviour plans and working toward updated curriculum that needs to be rolled out across the school can consume you and your team's important time.

I invite you to consider that a school is not a wellbeing, social service, business organisation but a teaching and learning organisation. It's a teaching and learning organisation that can greatly impact wellbeing, support our society and do so much more, but this happens through teaching and learning.

Putting positive behaviour plans into place, having great buildings and working on curriculum alignment are in service of teaching and learning.

In addition, teacher and student wellbeing serves teaching and learning. (We'll explore this soon.) And if your school has a wellbeing literacy you want to stick for all students, it's through teaching and learning that this happens.

In the era of overwhelm, there's a way to ensure teaching and learning are the school's full focus, and a structure in which to embed that will make it front and centre for everyone.

What are you busy with?

Considering your role, please list the top six things you're currently working on.

1.	2.	3.
4.	5.	6.

Question for consideration:
How many items on the list are focused on advancing teaching and learning across your school?

2. The endless chase

You're told that a specific list of teaching strategies creates high impact. The state has a new teaching and learning framework, and you can sign up to learn about that. You hear about students with trauma and want to ensure your school knows about this too. You read about a way to start each lesson, and you're thinking that your school should use that approach. You get a newsletter telling you AI is coming and the impact it will have on teaching and learning (it will!), and you think your leaders should know about this.

In fact, you might be hearing topics, titles or programs like these:

- The science of…
- High-impact…
- Evidence-based…
- Research-based…
- Direct instruction
- Explicit teaching
- Best practices
- Student-centred
- Science-based …

Or there might be new frameworks or mandates to learn about and implement…

Question for you:
What are the terms or phrases around teaching and learning that you know about or are hearing about? Maybe it's something the state, district or network is mandating, something you've read about, or the latest things you hear colleagues talking about.

Please record your top six here:

1.	2.
3.	4.
5.	6.

In this era, the chase is on. You can send out 'scouts' to take a program here or there and then try to figure out how to put it into your teaching team's practices. Those scouts can come back and present to your teaching team, hoping this new knowledge will spread. This approach can provide information on what's around but can lack depth of knowledge, details on how to set it up in the school's structure or guidance on how to effectively implement it.

You might even add this new learning to your school's teaching and learning framework (which might keep expanding) – a bit of this wellbeing framework here, a little bit of this student engagement piece here, a lesson plan format here; but you wonder if words on a document will turn into practice across the school.

The good news is there's a new way forward – a way that's broad enough to help you bring all of what you're already doing together, and simple and powerful enough for you to be able to easily see where new information fits and how to implement it in your school's practices. You can then replace 'chasing time' with the activities that will advance teaching and learning.

> 'So much of what we do complicates things.
> Unleash Learning is the simplest thing out there.
> It takes the complex and helps us use it easily.'
>
> *Assistant principal, Wodonga, Australia*

3. The challenge of time

If you've read this far, I commend you. In the era of overwhelm, time and attention are precious commodities. You probably have a million other items competing for your attention. In this new era, time for new learning, thinking and reflecting has shrunk. Programs that are speedy, webinars that are short, social media snippets or quick fixes are the new normal.

That's why it's going to take courage to lead learning in this new era, because to advance teaching and learning across your school will take time. In fact, it's going to take more than a half-day event to learn about and embed and require your leadership and team to build in the time and space that long-term engagement needs. Yet, once in place, it can give you more time, lower stress and create an impact that endures across your entire school.

 **Please take two minutes to write as much as you can as well as you can on the following question:**

How much time is currently devoted to schoolwide discussions about teaching and learning at your school and what do those discussions focus on?

4. Deciding on the 'right' embedded approach

Your team is deciding on the right teaching and learning approach or instructional framework to embed across your school. Or if you've got an established framework, you might be reflecting on it as you read this book. The framework is intended to help strengthen teaching and learning across your school/network/district, to create stability, focus and a shared approach – and if you conduct learning walks, support your team in being on the same page as to what to look for as high-quality teaching and learning in action.

This approach, depending on how effectively it's embedded (or will be embedded), **has the potential to shape everyone's thinking around teaching and learning** and the teaching and learning activities taking place. It can also shape how mentors and coaches work with educators.

The three kinds of educator thinking

In the era of overwhelm, there are three kinds of educator thinking to consider, one of which can help everyone stay agile, lower stress and expand impact. In fact, it will create an advanced level of teaching and learning across your school. The three kinds of thinking are:

1. Compliance thinking

This is the kind of thinking that happens when teaching and learning activities are mandated or people are just following prescribed teaching and learning operations. For example, a school might have a prescribed lesson plan template that all teachers must follow or a list of strategies educators must use.

In the era of overwhelm, compliance thinking might help create a shared approach across the school, but it can also teach people that teaching and learning just follow a script that comes from people outside of themselves, or there is a 'just tell me what to do' culture sets in because scripts are being provided by others.

But if you want your school to be innovative, support innovative teaching and learning practices, be responsive to change and help your team take on new information with ease, this is a type of thinking I want to invite you to avoid. To make these things happen in the era of overwhelm, a different kind of thinking is needed.

2. Strategies thinking

This is the kind of thinking where teachers see effective teaching as just teaching strategies to use or follow. It can happen when a school, network, district or state lists the strategies to use, or a researcher gives you his or her list of 'top' strategies (which often will change), with teachers picking the ones they like to use or simply trying to keep up with the latest thing.

This kind of thinking can lead to compliance or, worse, juggling. In fact, 'strategies thinking' can add to the overwhelm as educators see teaching and learning as strategies to 'just keep up with' or continue to juggle in their already full mental load.

Plus, from my own experience working with educators, without a set teaching and learning destination, it's possible some teachers don't know how to optimise the use of these strategies or, worse, can't even explain why they're using them.

3. Systems thinking

This kind of thinking happens when teachers know their teaching and learning destination and use a system to reach that destination. With this thinking, when educators learn new information, they're able to put it into the system, rather than automatically jump to something new or try to keep up with the latest thing.

Systems thinking can lower a teacher's stress, increase their effectiveness and help them stay innovative and responsive in a disruptive and changing world. It can bring a sense of order to avoid a sense of chaos. That's because they have a framework of understanding of how things fit together and how to use this framework to reach a specific destination. When new information comes to them, they can put it into their system and use it easily and seamlessly to get a specific kind of outcome, without the overwhelm.

This kind of thinking takes time and requires a specific structure to be embedded, maintained and supported across your school. But once it sticks, change lasts. It's the kind of thinking needed in the new era of overwhelm.

Chapter 2

Leading Learning in the Era of Overwhelm

The delivery model of education – there is another way

In the delivery model of education, the goal is to 'deliver' information to students, who are seen as empty vessels to be filled up (Freire, 1975). If you've ever sat through a webinar or a professional learning session where the presenter does most of the talking, you know the model.

In this model, the era of overwhelm can result in your school trying to keep up with learning new ways to 'deliver' information to students through a mandated lesson format; by focusing on this or that teaching strategy; by embedding a new technology; or by using a new lesson template formula or assessment process.

Over the years, students who have experienced this model have told me they learned how to 'play the game of school' by focusing on getting through assignments, keeping their head down, and doing what the teacher wanted. Many of these students also explain they didn't feel like they remembered much or were personally affected by what was being taught. Or worse, they simply learned to comply (Wink, 2000).

If the delivery of information is what is needed, the internet would have made us very smart people. If teaching and learning is just about task completion, we could just put material online for students to complete and allow students to stay home.

Without realising it, the advancement you seek might just be more 'delivery' in action. Or as one colleague often tells me when we discuss many teaching and learning reforms – 'same wine, different bottle.'

'Delivery' is so ingrained in our profession that I hear it spoken about wherever I go. It often sounds something like this:

- I 'delivered' the lesson by…
- Our team 'delivers' our wellbeing curriculum by…
- I 'delivered' the literacy workshop…
- Our school 'delivers' teaching programs through…

But you're after something different. You want to support the kind of teaching and learning across your entire school (not just for a few teachers here and there) that leads to positive behavioural change, to transformational understandings (for all students), and to learning that stays with students and that they can use for the rest of their lives.

To advance that kind of teaching and learning schoolwide, the first thing to do is interrupt that story. To do this, I'd like to ask you an important question.

The story in your head

The delivery model is so engrained in people's notions of teaching and learning that even with a teaching and learning framework in place for your school and mandated specific 'strategies' to be used, you might find that people quickly revert to the delivery approach (DeJean, 2015). That's because even with your teaching and learning framework, many people across your school are facilitating teaching and learning based on their deeply engrained past experiences and beliefs (DeJean, 2020).

Let's try something. Answer the following question in the space provided:

What do you mean when you think about teaching and learning?

You might also consider asking a few members of your team (teachers, leaders, coaches, mentors) the same question. In fact, at your next leadership meeting I invite you to ask everyone to record their answer to the question and then share the answers to see if your team has a common language, if 'delivery' is the default vision and if their explanations mirror activities taking place across the school.

unleash-learning.com

Want more?

Scan this QR code and get instant access to our Unleash Learning TV episode ('6 leadership team questions to ask about teaching and learning across your school') with a free workbook.

Use both at your next leadership meeting.

Creating a common language

To move past the delivery of information, stay focused in the era of overwhelm and advance teaching and learning across your school, I'm going to be inviting you to embed a structure around your school. This structure will include a shared language with specific definitions around high-quality teaching and learning. This common language will become your approach that gets to the heart of teaching and learning and will endure because it's flexible and large enough for new initiatives and strategies to be easily integrated into it.

The common language I'm speaking about isn't focused on teaching strategies or standards. (They have their place, but not here.) This language isn't focused on subject-specific content or terms people know about or are using. It's a language that will shape a shared understanding of the kind of teaching and learning that will lead to long-term learning for everyone. It's a language focused on a structure for learning. Let's call it a system. It involves a perspective called *systems thinking*.

It's language that will:

- inform your entire school's thinking about teaching and learning
- create stability and alignment
- help everyone optimise what they already do
- get to the crux of people's thinking
- incorporate the strategies, programs and framework your school uses
- build systems thinking
- help embed a structure that doesn't change, even when things do.

To make this happen, and create a lasting impact, especially in the era of overwhelm, it's important you do that in a new way.

The old way vs the new way for advancing teaching and learning

To help understand this, let's imagine you're the mayor of a very small town. When the town was small, there were so few cars on the road or people on the sidewalks, there was no need for stop signs or traffic lights. Things moved well and people were able to make their own way without a set, agreed-upon structure.

But now the town is starting to grow. With it, traffic is slowing and gridlock is occurring. You and your team know your leadership is needed to put the right structure in place to help the town move easily and seamlessly (and safely!). The state or country in which your town is located might impact how people participate in your town, but you focus on what you can control and decide to act.

But without careful consideration you might find that putting in the wrong things (too many stop lights, for instance, or intersections that are built poorly) can cause the same problems they're designed to solve.

That's because in this case the **form** did not create the desired **function**.

What's the form? In the case of your school, it's the structure that has been created by your school, network, district, state or society. This form might be explicit – you must teach this way, everyone must take this exam, etc. Or it might be implicit – that is, people might not be able to name the form, but it's impacting how they operate.

What's the function? It's how your team participates inside the structure: thinks, engages, reflects, teaches or leads. In fact, sometimes teachers are using the delivery model based on the form that's been established in the school, network or district.

 **Please read this statement out loud three times:**

The form creates the function!

The form creates the function!

The form creates the function!

If you're working to advance teaching and learning across your school in the era of overwhelm, it's important to first put the kind of form (or structure) into place that helps everyone participate in teaching and learning. Once that structure is in place, your leadership will be needed to:

- keep everyone focused on the structure (which, in the era of overwhelm, will take consistency!)
- support how everyone (leaders, new and experienced teachers, mentors, coaches and more) positively functions inside of it.

I refer to these structures as the old way vs the new way. Let's look at what I'm calling 'the old way', and then we'll dive into the new structures, which I'm calling 'the new way'.

The old way

This way can be inconsistent, ineffective and inefficient in that it's short-term and focused on individual teachers or small groups. In most schools, it tends to look and feel:

- siloed
- piecemeal
- as if everyone is trying to keep up
- short-term
- like herding cats
- like the school is chasing the latest new thing.

The new way

This way can advance teaching and learning consistently, effectively and efficiently. In schools this new way:

- gets to the crux of everyone's thinking
- is mission-driven
- can evolve with the times
- once in place, will last for years to come
- is broader and more holistic
- is long-term
- helps a school optimise everything it does
- creates common language with shared definitions
- lowers stress and mental load with consistent and effective systems of thinking, streamlining teaching efforts.

Let's explore how to do just that.

A new way forward

To create stability in this new era, I'm going to invite you to choose a new way forward for you and your school by embedding a very specific structure (the form) which includes an ambitious teaching and learning mission that stays the same – even when curriculum and content change.

I'm then going to invite you to embed a simple but powerful teaching and learning system that empowers teachers and school leaders to reach that mission and optimise everything they do. This system will require a common language around core activities needed to reach that mission.

For example, this system includes a shared understanding of the plan teachers use for all their lessons, the kind of student engagement that helps make learning stick for everyone, ways to set up the learning environment to create the conditions required to reach the mission, and how both teacher and student wellbeing serve teaching and learning.

Your leadership team, new and experienced teachers and instructional leaders might use the system in different ways. But with a clear teaching and learning mission and a system that supports learning embedded across your school, you can create schoolwide alignment and a shared understanding of high-quality teaching and learning that doesn't change. Even when things do.

If you use it effectively (I know you will!), you'll then be able to help your school take on new information, easily.

Taking on new information with ease

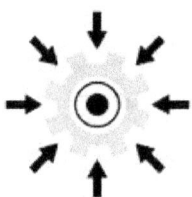

A living system is a learning system (Wheatley, 2017). That is, a system must take on new information to evolve, adapt and thrive. But in the era of overwhelm, new information can flood your team. That's why I'm inviting you to embed an open-sourced system – a system that's broad enough to bring together all that you do and open enough to help your team take on new information with ease.

For instance, when a new wellbeing initiative comes to your school, with the right mission and system already in place, your team will quickly see where it fits and how it enhances your teaching and learning objectives. Teachers might adjust their classroom set-up based on their knowledge of student wellbeing, strengthen how they link content to the lives of their students, and use their deep understanding of engagement to enhance wellbeing for all their students.

With a schoolwide teaching and learning mission and this open-system approach, your school can use this new information to continue to advance teaching and learning.

How do you do this? I'm glad you asked. It's time to delve into exactly what that means, so let's explore that now!

Part 2
Systems Thinking in the Era of Overwhelm

'Goals are for people who care about winning once.
Systems are for people who care about
winning repeatedly.'
James Clear

Chapter 3

Embedding a Shared Teaching and Learning Mission

 One day, on a very windy morning, I was standing on a cliff overlooking Sydney Harbour. There wasn't a cloud in the sky, but strong winds were blowing in different directions, and large swells were moving across the water.

The waves on the harbour were large, and many of the boats sailing on it looked like they were being tossed in different directions. At times it appeared that the winds and waves were in charge, not the captains of the ships.

But one boat was moving forward in what appeared to be a definite and strong direction.

That ship seemed to have a clearly defined mission. When the wind blew in an unexpected new way or a wave hit the ship, it kept a steady course. The captain didn't seem distracted but appeared to be making a few slight adjustments. He seemed to have a clear focus on the intended destination and to know how to use the entire ship to reach it.

It's an image I think of often.

Supporting the craft

For schools, those winds and waves are speeding up. They might be new curriculum mandates, the latest district, network or state framework, or a focus on student wellbeing or on 'keeping up' with the advancement of technology – the **what** teachers need to teach and the tools they need to use. Here are examples of the **what** of teaching and learning:

Teaching strategy	Prior knowledge	Seating plans
Notetaking	Teaching standard	Teacher wellbeing
Content	Learning intention	Technology
Teacher wellbeing	The lesson plan	A skill set

The **what** is important but it's subject to change. And it can be part of the flood of information your team is dealing with.

But because you want to advance teaching and learning across your school, I suggest you focus on what doesn't change, even when other things do. In the case of teaching and learning, it's the **how**: how teachers and leaders **use** the tools (strategies, content and more) to reach a specific destination.

The **how** are the activities, actions or ways a teacher uses a strategy or has all students engage with content in intentional and planned-for ways to get to the specific destination or outcome. The **how** is the craft.

Great sailors, artists, athletes, orators or educators might have natural talents. But they've also studied and, in many cases, mastered their craft.

What's craft?

- Craft is the skill.
- Craft is talent put into action.
- Craft is the way someone puts knowledge into action.
- Craft is the way sailors effectively sail the ship.
- Craft is systems thinking in action.

For teachers, craft might look like knowing about a strategy or content (the **what**) and **how** they intentionally and systematically use their craft (their metaphorical ship) to reach their intended outcome.

If you want to advance teaching and learning across your school and optimise what your team is already doing, it's important to embed a structure to help everyone think about and strengthen their **how**. That starts with the right mission. It's a mission that most schools don't have.

The difference between your school's mission and having a teaching and learning mission

You want teaching and learning to be your school's number-one priority. You want to help advance it across your school. You're working to create a structure that will support the ways everyone thinks about teaching and learning – and will last for years to come.

That's why a clear mission is so critical.

I'm guessing your school already has a mission. It might be found on your school signage or website or in program guides or your staff manual.

I'm going to suggest that your school's mission is your **why** – why your school does what it does, or what outcomes your school is working toward.

It might come in many forms, but is likely to have words connected to these ideas:

- empowering students
- creating the future
- helping students reach their full potential
- striving for excellence.

That school mission, if used well, has the potential to shape the activities of everyone at your school.

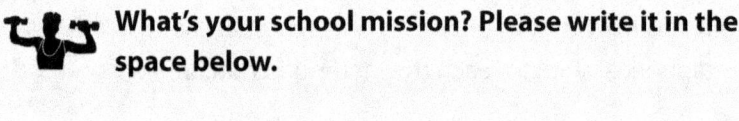 **What's your school mission? Please write it in the space below.**

As you think about the activities, thinking and focus of teaching and learning at your school, I invite you to consider embedding an ambitious teaching and learning mission. In the era of overwhelm, the right teaching and learning mission can help your entire school stay laser-focused, create schoolwide alignment and optimise what they do.

It's essential that this teaching and learning mission is clear, front and centre and easy for everyone to talk about and understand. It also needs to be ambitious to make it a stretch goal – to help your school continue to dream big. It's a mission that won't change, even when things do. The right teaching and learning mission combined with the right system (we'll talk about that shortly) has the power to replace (or interrupt) the 'delivery' model of education and support everyone across your school as they consider the following:

Teaching strategies	The classroom	The pacing of the lesson
Content	Technology	Wellbeing
How they open or close a lesson	All parts of their metaphorical ship	And much more!

The teaching and learning mission to embed

School leaders and teachers I talk to want teaching and learning to cause all students to be able to:

- experience positive behavioural change
- experience transformative understandings
- use the important lessons, content, skills or ideas they learn
- take what they learn in every class and use it for the rest of their lives
- go on to live bigger and better lives
- transcend limits
- remember that the school made a difference and retain what they have learned for the rest of their lives.

If any of these statements connect with you, too, I'm going to suggest you know the destination you're after. You want to make learning stick for everyone.

Teaching strategies, contents, exams, assignments and more are all tools your school uses to make this happen.

That's why I'm going to invite you to embed this as your school's teaching and learning mission. This mission is brief, specific and intentional and destined to focus on students' learning that lasts. It is short but powerful. It is:

 **Please read this out loud:**

> Make learning stick for everyone.

To understand this teaching and learning mission, let's examine its two parts:

Part 1: To make learning stick

In a delivery model of education, the goal is to 'deliver' content or help students get through assignments. But this mission invites everyone across your school to think about a different kind of outcome, one that causes long-term learning that lasts.

To make this happen, everyone will need to be supported with the understanding of what science suggests makes this happen (we'll get to this, soon) and a shared system (that's coming up, too!) they'll use to make that happen. This structure/system, if implemented effectively, can support systems thinking across your school. That is, leaders and educators will be thinking about every choice they're making, how those pieces fit together and how they're using the entire system to reach that mission.

Part 2: For everyone

In the most traditional interpretation of the delivery model of education, who the students are doesn't matter, as they are seen as empty vessels to fill up with information. But this part of the mission changes that view, inviting everyone across your school to think about who students are in important ways and helping them consider how to use that knowledge to make learning stick for everyone. This perspective can inform teachers about how to understand who their students are, and then use that knowledge to connect all students to the content and class and find ways to create inclusive participation and a collective sense of belonging in every lesson. Why is this important? Because as you'll see shortly, these are core components of what makes learning stick for everyone.

But to make this happen effectively will require more than embedding this teaching and learning mission across your school. It will also require everyone to have a shared understanding of what makes learning stick for everyone. It's time to explore that now.

Chapter 4

What Makes Learning Stick for Everyone

> 'Learning can be a box that once opened, changes everything.'
>
> *Dr William DeJean, Unleash Learning*

To use this teaching and learning mission effectively, it will need to be embedded in the right locations (we'll explore that later) and you will need to ensure there's a common understanding with easy-to-use language embedded across your school. To do that, let's turn to science.

The way I'm about to explain the science comes from every book and research article I've read, every education course I've written and taught at university level, every piece of curriculum I've developed and from every educational researcher with whom I've studied or worked. It also comes from working with educators in their classrooms and leaders who are leading learning across their schools.

Before we go any further, it's important to think about what the research *doesn't say* makes learning stick. Research in the field of education doesn't say:

- just put content online
- the educator's job is to 'deliver' information to learners
- have learners just fill in a worksheet
- the educator should speak for most of the time to make learning stick.

At its core, here's what the research does say (DeJean, 2020; Marzano, 2007; Neisser, 1967):

 Please say these two statements out loud as if you're explaining them to someone else:

1. **Intentional** and **planned-for** student engagement is what makes learning stick.
2. There are specific things both the teacher and students need to be **doing** that help make this happen.

By *intentional*, I mean that every choice an educator makes:

- is done with the mission of getting learning to stick, for everyone
- is done on purpose
- is enacted with reason
- can be justified, and
- is based on an understanding of what it takes to make learning stick for everyone.

💪 When you write it you learn it!

In 30 words or less, how would you explain what intentional engagement is?

Then, please read your response to someone on your leadership team.

By *planned-for*, I mean:

- The educator plans lessons in a targeted way.
- During lesson planning, the educator focuses on learning rather than teaching.
- The educator understands what kinds of engagement make learning stick for all learners.
- During the lesson-planning process, the educator strategically embeds targeted strategies throughout to ensure *all* students are consistently engaged in specific and targeted ways.

💪 When you draw it, you learn it!

In the space below, please draw three to five images that represent what planned-for engagement means to you.

Then, please share your response with someone on your leadership team.

What are the things the educator and students need to be doing? We'll talk about this soon, but first, let's talk about why intentional student engagement is the key to making learning stick for everyone. To do that, I need to take you to the gym.

Think like a personal trainer

If you want to gain muscle, you go to a personal trainer because he or she is an expert in what it takes for you to gain muscle. That person knows that for you to gain muscle the trainer must intentionally get you to lift the weights in specific and targeted ways throughout the entire workout.

The personal trainer knows, based on the science, that there are specific fibres in muscles that must be activated and that by putting specific weights into your hands and ensuring you lift the weights in specific and targeted ways and for specific amounts of time, the personal trainer can get specific fibres firing.

It's the fibres *firing* that activates the fibres to expand; and expansion of the fibres is what gets the muscle to unleash to its fullest potential.

Personal trainers make every decision about their work based on this fact.

Because of this, they don't do the following:

- talk to you throughout the session about what it takes to gain muscle
- show you movies about what it takes to gain muscle
- read articles to you about what it takes to gain muscle
- lift weights and have you watch them do it for the majority of the session.

What they don't do is *deliver* information to you. Rather, they get you to lift the weights for most of the time in intentional and planned-for ways.

In fact, they know that each minute you're with them is precious time, so they ensure the majority of your time together is spent on lifting the weights. They're so knowledgeable about what it takes to gain muscle that they control the kinds of weights you use and the pacing of the weightlifting to get the exact outcome they are after.

If they were just about *delivering* information, they know they could be replaced by apps, YouTube videos and other internet *delivery* platforms. The great trainers are the ones that consistently get outcomes for their clients.

In learning, we like to say: 'Neurons that fire together wire together.'

The reason intentional and planned-for student engagement – or Lifting the Weights – is so important is that it gets neurons 'firing and wiring' together. It's the firing and wiring that get learning to stick. To see if this is true, here's something you can do at your next staff meeting.

I didn't learn a subject until I taught it

I often start school workshops or the launch of Unleash Learning at a school with this specific statement and ask people to raise their hands if they find it to be a true statement. You're welcome to use this statement at your next staff meeting and see if the response is the same.

> The statement: **I didn't learn a subject until I taught the subject.**

No matter the location (United States, Australia, rural, suburban or city) or the kind of school (private, public, primary, middle or high school), most of the hands will go into the air. And if you want to make learning stick for everyone, it's an important statement to remember.

It means these talented people spent years in university, attending classes, completing assignments and possibly 'sitting' exams on their subject and our profession. But it wasn't until they *taught* the subject that they learned the subject.

It's a reminder that if you want to get learning to stick for students across your school, it's essential that *all* of the students are Lifting the Weights in intentional and planned-for ways throughout most of each lesson.

It's more important than ever that students are Lifting the Weights as it's been reported (Gross, 2017) that 'in Australia, many students are consistently disengaged in class: as many as 40 per cent are unproductive in any given year. And that nearly one in four students are compliant but quietly disengaged' (p. 3).

What exactly do I mean by Lifting the Weights? I mean the moments when *all* students do the following:

Write *it*	Speak *it*	Explain *it*	Question *it*
Draw *it*	Become *it*	Discuss *it*	Teach *it*
Summarise *it*	Repeat *it*	Read *it*	Dance *it*

At its core, every effective literacy or instructional strategy addresses these processes, because these are the actions that help make learning stick for everyone. This teacher's comment highlights that engagement:

> 'Before this, the person who knew it the best was me, because I was teaching it.
> Now the way I plan has changed.

> I plan for who is going to lift the weights and ask myself, what are my kids going to **do** with *it*?
>
> *Karen Corbet, Western Australia*

You might also notice what the list doesn't say. It doesn't say show students a film clip, speak to them the entire time, have one person do all the talking, just do the work online, fill out a worksheet, or complete a multiple-choice test.

The weights I'm speaking about are targeted and specific and ensure that learning sticks for everyone. That's why I want you to remember the items in the chart, because they are the actions educators need to facilitate all students actively 'doing' across your school for most of the time. That's what makes learning sick. But to do this, it's essential that all students in every classroom across your school are Lifting the Weights toward the right objective of the lesson.

Let's call it the *it or its* of your lesson. We'll get to that shortly.

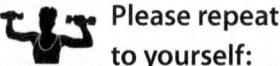 **Please repeat this statement three times, out loud to yourself:**

1. It's *all* about Lifting the Weights!
2. It's *all* about Lifting the Weights!
3. It's *all* about Lifting the Weights!

Optimising teaching and learning

How can this understanding help optimise teaching and learning at your school? The most important way is when teachers across your school, network or district understand what makes learning stick and use the system we'll discuss soon. At that point, they'll think about how they're using the tools they already have.

Here's an example. Let's say your school has notetaking as a 'strategy' you want all teachers to use. They might be having students take notes in many of their classes. But when teachers understand that it's all about Lifting the Weights, they'll consider how to *use* this tool to make learning stick for everyone. For example, you might see teachers asking their students to take notes (writing *it*), but they'll add additional weightlifting.

This might include the following intentional and planned-for actions:

- partners teaching their notes to each other
- everyone reading a summary of their notes at the end of the lesson
- everyone explaining the most important item in their notes to multiple students in the class
- students drawing a few images based on their notes and then explaining their drawings to their table partner
- students explaining to each other how taking notes is helping to make their own learning stick.

This isn't engagement for engagement's sake. It's engagement on the right 'fibres' your teaching team wants to make stronger, or in this case, making learning stick. Knowing the exact 'fibres' found in a lesson, unit or course is the next way to advance teaching and learning across your school. To do that, educators need to know the *it* or *its*.

Knowing the *it*

Personal trainers know the exact fibres they're working to get firing. The same is true for educators, who need to be just as targeted with the 'learning fibres' they're getting 'firing and wiring' for *all* their students.

To do this, teachers must ensure *all* of their students are Lifting the Weights on the exact *it* of their lesson, unit or subject. What's the *it* of the lesson?

Specifically, it's *what* a teacher wants to stick for everyone – in other words, the learning objectives. These might be:

- key vocabulary
- a main idea
- a core concept
- a specific skill set.

If educators across your school want learning to stick, they must be laser-focused on what they want to stick for all learners. The same is true for the meeting you run, the instructional leadership activities you lead or any time your teaching team sees you modelling learning.

For example, if we were working together, here are a few *it(s)* that I'd want to stick for you:

- The era of overwhelm
- The delivery model of education
- Intentional and planned-for engagement is what makes learning stick.
- It's all about Lifting the Weights.
- 'Neurons that wire together fire together.'
- Form creates the function.

To get this to stick, I'd engage you in writing, speaking, teaching, repeating, explaining and summarising these *it(s)* repeatedly in numerous ways, until they stick.

> 'The gold in the Unleash Learning System™ is teachers actually understanding what the *it* is.'
>
> *Mary Chiodo-Jennings, Campus Principal, Copperfield College, Unleash Learning Certified Teacher*

The most important questions to ask

This is a real scenario. We just completed the first learning walk as part of our Unleash Learning Year 2 activities in a large, suburban, multicampus, 7–12 school in Melbourne, Australia, which included teachers and members of the leadership team. We went into the conference room and began to debrief the observations from an Unleash Learning perspective. To start, I asked everyone to write in their notes their overall observations.

When they had finished writing and sharing that writing with their table partner, I asked a few people to share out loud. Alex simply said, 'Students across our school are all in the same, passive position.'

'What's the same, passive position?' I asked.

To show the position, Alex went to the conference table, hunched over a piece of paper and pretended he was writing. He then got up and went to another area of the conference table, grabbed his laptop and hunched as if he were working on a computer.

'Why is this a problem?' I questioned.

'Because we need to get them to lift the weights in multiple ways throughout each lesson. We need to get them speaking, writing, explaining, teaching, discussing in intentional ways on the right *it* or *its* of our lesson. It might mean classrooms would be a bit louder, we'd see movement, and a different kind of pacing to the lesson would be happening.'

You don't need Alex to come to your school to talk about this (although he's now an Unleash Learning Certified Teacher!). You simply need three questions. In fact, you might consider writing these three questions on a sheet of paper and hanging them on your office or staff-room wall or somewhere else where your leadership and teaching team will see them.

The questions are as follows:

 **Please read these questions out loud.**

1. Who is Lifting the Weights?
2. For how long are they Lifting the Weights?
3. In how many different ways are they Lifting the Weights?

To understand these three questions, let's consider what you or your teaching team might be thinking about each one.

Question 1: Who is Lifting the Weights?

 This question invites everyone to pay attention to who. That is, who exactly is Lifting the Weights? In fact, it might cause educators to think about the identities and backgrounds of students in different ways. For example:

- In collaboration, are the boys doing all the talking?
- Are our multilingual students speaking, writing and explaining?
- What about our students of colour?
- How can the teacher and students work to distribute the weights to everyone?

If your teaching and learning mission is to make learning stick for everyone, answering this question will help your entire school see all the students and consider how to actively distribute the weights to everyone.

Question 2: For how long are they Lifting the Weights?

If you go to the gym to gain muscle, it's important you're lifting weights most of your time there. Yes, it's important to create pauses between each set, but to make the muscle expand, you need to lift weights for the majority of the time you're at the gym to get the wiring and firing to happen.

The same is true if you want to make learning stick for everyone. That is, we need students Lifting the Weights in intentional and planned-for ways through most of the lesson.

This question can help you and your entire team see for how long students are Lifting the Weights and consider how to increase the weightlifting time in each class session.

Question 3: In how many ways are they Lifting the Weights?

The reason many teachers say they didn't learn a subject until they taught it is because teaching requires them to Lift the Weights in multiple ways. That is, they might be:

writing *it*	explaining *it*	teaching *it*
drawing *it*	summarising *it*	and more

That's why the subject sticks for them. It's the multiple ways they're Lifting the Weights that makes learning sticky.

This third question will help your team consider the *it* or *its* of the lesson and examine in how many ways *all* students are Lifting the Weights with a focus on the right *it* or *its*. That is, how many times does the teacher intentionally facilitate *all* students speaking *it*, writing *it*, explaining *it* and more throughout each part of the lesson?

These three questions can help your school consider one part of what it takes to reach your teaching and learning mission. They all relate to the idea of *engagement*.

But as a reminder, science suggests it takes more than just engagement to make learning stick. It takes what I call a **doing system**, a system that can help advance teaching and learning – in other words, bringing together what you're already doing and, in the era of overwhelm, helping your team easily and seamlessly take on new information.

What's the system? It's time to find out.

Consider this action before reading the next chapter:

Individually (or ideally as a leadership team) walk around the campus or campuses and visit as many classrooms as possible. In each classroom ask yourself the three questions:

1. Who is Lifting the Weights?

2. For how long are they Lifting the Weights?

3. In how many different ways are they Lifting the Weights?

Chapter 5

The System That Makes Learning Stick for Everyone

'Simplify to amplify.'

Felecia Etienne

You're working to advance teaching and learning across your school/network/district. You might create (or have created) a teaching and learning framework to inform and influence how everyone engages with teaching and learning. In fact, you want the framework to help teachers strengthen their craft in ways that cause long-term learning for all students.

But you might find that the teaching and learning documents you create (or plan to create) don't fully translate to the advancement you hoped for, or worse, the ways they're translated by your school cause more 'delivery' in action or create more compliance thinking. There are many reasons why this may be the case. But here are two to consider:

Reason #1: How learning sticks

We often don't learn in facts, figures, and statistics. We learn best when we are engaged with content in ways designed to support memory and promote learning (Lakoff & Johnson, 2008). This is true for you and me, students across your school and your teaching and leadership teams.

Lists of popular teaching strategies, standards documents, and teaching and learning frameworks can get in the way of learning content, in addition to being challenging to apply.

This may have been true in any era, but in the era of overwhelm all of this can cause more overload. It's why I talk about Lifting the Weights, piloting a ship, and keys, all designed to help complex concepts stick for you and your school community and to do so within a system that focuses on making learning stick for everyone.

Reason #2: Praxis

I define praxis as theory in action. There's often a large gap between theory and, in this case, teaching and learning practices. For instance, there might be highly accomplished researchers in the field of education, but translating that research into practice might not be effective. That could be the case because the researchers' expertise is in research and not in pedagogical practice. Or people across your school, network, district or state might be well versed in a collective teaching and learning framework, but translating this into effective practice might be a challenge (Schmoker, 2006).

That's why the era of overwhelm is calling for a new way forward. And that new way helps you create a system that's easy to understand and can be turned into the collective praxis of your school.

What a system can do

An effective system provides a framework for organising our thinking. It helps easily capture an idea, an approach or a way of participating. With the right system, your school can take in new information (i.e., new standards, strategies, research) and place it in your existing system.

Over time the system becomes your school's approach. When things are not working the way you want, you know where to make slight adjustments and find your true north again. The system helps your school stay laser-focused, empowered and confident in your approach, no matter what changes come your way.

It can also become an island of sanity (Wheatley, 2024). That is, it can approach the era of overwhelm in ways that you can control, help your school stay focused and lower school stress and overload. For good.

As a school with a system

- You stay focused on your mission to make learning stick for everyone.
- You have an approach that makes learning stick.
- You achieve schoolwide alignment because everyone is on the same page with a shared language and direction.
- Leaders and new and experienced teachers can explain the teaching and learning choices they are making based on the system.
- Your school learns more, and you can confidently adapt and incorporate new knowledge into the system in an organised fashion.
- You feel empowered by being able to make learning stick for everyone.
- The sense of a mental overload and overwhelm can be lowered.

The system we're about to explore is a simple but powerful teaching and learning system that empowers teachers and leaders across your school to optimise everything they do. It does this by providing a common language with clear definitions that won't change, even when many other things do. It's the ship that everyone at your school, network or district will use to reach your school's teaching and learning destination.

The Unleash Learning System™

I began Part 2 of this book by introducing the image of a ship and the actions of its captain. I use that analogy to highlight the various elements that affect smooth sailing and the critical expertise of its captain in keeping the ship on its charted course.

The captain uses specific systems to steer the ship toward its specified destination. You and your team are not steering a ship, but you are steering a course where the destination is the objective of making learning stick for everyone. I am going to describe a system that contains six fundamental keys to reach this destination. The research supporting this system comes from the fields of education, literacy, cognitive science, neuroscience, multicultural education and positive psychology. It also comes from real-world experiences that include working with educators in their classrooms, supporting school leaders and actually teaching in schools and in a variety of education courses at the university level.

The keys, working together, unlock the potential of your school's teaching and learning mission: To get learning to stick for everyone. Once everyone at your school knows what these keys are and how to use them effectively, no matter the ship (online, face-to-face, blended learning), you'll collectively sail effectively.

It's time to share with you the keys in the Unleash Learning System™ that gets you to your destination. As I describe each key, I invite you to be thinking: how does this connect to what we do here, this standard or that state-wide framework? What is our school doing well. In other words, what are we doing that represents expert sailing? Or consider: 'What part of my ship needs help to advance teaching and learning schoolwide?'

It's time to share the keys in the Unleash Learning System™!

The Key of Teacher

In the delivery model of education, who a teacher is doesn't matter. That's because, at the most basic level, the teacher is simply responsible for 'delivery' of information to passive students. That might be why in many teaching and learning books, frameworks, teacher education courses or standards, who the teacher is may hardly be mentioned. But your school wants learning to stick for everyone. And for this reason and many more, who the teacher is matters. A lot.

Here are a few reasons why:

1. We teach who we are

Parker J. Palmer (1998) suggests that 'Good teaching cannot be reduced to technique. Good teaching come from the identity and integrity of the teacher' (p. 4). Maxine Greene (1988) says that 'only a teacher in search of his or her own freedom can inspire students to search for their own freedom' (p. 14). Researchers, thought leaders and my own doctoral dissertation research all point to an important reality – that who an educator is influences and shapes their teaching and learning beliefs and practices.

Those practices are shaped by a teacher's life history, background, identities (race, gender, language, nationality, sexual orientation), wellbeing and their own experience with school.

Case studies have pointed to the conclusion that the manner in which a person teaches is, to a great extent, directly related to how they were taught (Brookfield, 2017). It's one reason why the delivery model is so hard to change! In other words, we tend to teach like we experienced schooling.

Here's another example.

If you or teachers at your school were excluded in any way (maybe because of your sexual orientation, race, religion or faith, or family makeup), you might be keenly aware of the importance of inclusion; and therefore, it would inform your approach. While the standards, frameworks or materials you use might not talk about this, your teaching might be informed by these experiences, and you might strive to create an environment where everyone participates and feels like they belong.

I've also met educators who, knowing themselves, worked on getting more organised, taking care of their health and setting healthy lifestyle boundaries, consequently reporting that in the process their effectiveness as educators increased.

2. A teacher's *why* matters

A teacher's *why*, or their intentions for being an educator or leader, is the greatest power they have, whether with a group of students in a school or with professionals in the world of work.

If you know your *why* – that is, your real reason for teaching a subject or grade level, for example, or leading learning across your school or schools – you'll know the main reasons why you're doing your work, and that why will provide the fuel you need as you're dealing with everything that's on your plate.

Here's an example. Maybe you're leading learning across your school because your own schooling opened doors of possibility for your own life and you want to pass that on to other students. When you lead learning from that place, learners can feel that commitment from you, without you saying a word. The technology, audience or content might change, but your reasons and commitment to teaching or leading learning do not.

Your *why* has the potential to keep everyone focused and lessen any distractions and will translate for your learners into a recognisable passion and commitment.

Now, there's one more thing you need to know about your *why*. Hopefully it will change.

With more information, more time in the profession, more exposure to a variety of learners and audiences, or more information, you will begin to see your work through fresh eyes. New perspectives might include social justice, becoming a change-agent, equity, inclusion or wellbeing for everyone. Keep it changing. Let it evolve. Let it inspire you. Let it help make the world better.

Hopefully one part of your *why* won't change: the intention to get learning to stick, for everyone.

Students remember the teacher

Over the years I've asked people to tell me about their favourite teacher. What they describe to me often starts with who the teacher was. That is, they remember the teacher's passion, wisdom, encouragement, excitement and other characteristics. In fact, some of these people can describe the teacher in detail but can't remember the subject they taught or the assignments that were part of the class. What they remember is who the teacher was and the impact that person had on their life.

>  **Please read this key's description out loud.**
>
> A self-reflective teacher matters. Teachers who are connected to their meaning and purpose, who know their strengths, who know how to focus on their health and wellbeing and who understand how their identities affect their teaching, have powerful knowledge that makes learning stick for all students.

Once embedded, your school (or schools) might use the Key of Teacher in the following ways:

What leaders do:

- Leaders conduct staff meetings that help everyone to stay connected to their own meaning and purpose.
- Leaders understand which character strengths they overplay or underplay.
- Leaders help everyone develop their own wellbeing literacy in service of teaching and learning.
- Mentors mentor others while also creating a life they love.

What teachers do:

- Teachers understand the connection between who they are and how they teach.

- Teachers create time to reflect on their own lives.
- Everyone strengthens their own organisational skills.
- People give up the need to please as an overall approach to life.
- New teachers learn to set reasonable priorities for their time.
- Everyone thinks about their own identities (race, gender, languages, backgrounds, sexual orientation, nationalities and more).
- Teachers examine their own shadow beliefs.
- People take care of themselves, including getting more sleep.
- People hire a coach or get therapy when it can be helpful.
- Everyone is able to explain how they are *using* the Key of Teacher to make learning stick for everyone.

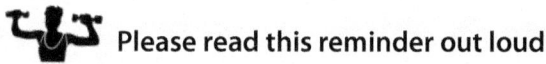 **Please read this reminder out loud:**

Teaching strategies are not the teaching and learning destination but are in service of the system that helps an educator reach it.

Evaluate your school's (or schools') use of this key

1. Looking at the key's description, explain which aspect of that description is your school's (or schools') strength.

2. What aspect of this key's description would help move the school from good to great?

The Key of Engagement

If your school's teaching and learning mission is to make learning stick for everyone, I hope I've convinced you that if you want to make learning stick for everyone, full student engagement matters. Remember, it's all about Lifting the Weights! To get the most out of this key, there are a few essentials.

1. All means all

The conductor of a symphony conducts to ensure that the entire orchestra plays together. That's how a symphony is created. The conductor thinks about everyone as one group, rather than as individual players. That doesn't mean the conductor ignores the individuals. Rather, he or she is thinking about conducting for the entire group, knowing that everyone must play their instruments at the right time if there's to be a symphony.

In the delivery model, an educator might ask one or two students for their opinions or ideas while the rest of the class passively sits and listens (if they're listening at all!). Or during a staff meeting the leader might ask one person to share while everyone sits quietly.

To make the most of the idea of Lifting the Weights, it's essential that *all* students in every classroom are involved.

That's why *all* means *all*.

To make sure that learning sticks for everyone, it's essential that *all* students are Lifting the Weights, all the time, not just one person at a time or the same few people. For example, rather than calling on just one person, a teacher using this key might ask a question and have *everyone* record their response, then share with their table partner about it, and then ask a few people to share their responses – while everyone takes notes on what they hear being said.

There are multiple ways to use this key – more suggested ways are coming soon – but first remember: *all* means *all*! When this key is embedded across your school, your team will be working to find ways to pass the weights out to everyone.

2. It must be the right kind of engagement

Remember, intentional and planned-for student engagement is what makes learning stick. Engagement for engagement's sake does not. The kind of engagement we're talking about is the kind that makes sure all students are Lifting the Weights on the objective, the exact *it* that a teacher wants to stick.

Personal trainers target the kind of engagement that gets clients' muscles to work, in essence to make the muscle learning stick. When teachers are targeted regarding the *it* of their lesson and get all students Lifting the Weights toward the objective throughout the lesson, the teacher is working proactively to make learning stick.

3. Learners must lift the weights in multiple ways

You don't go to the gym and use the same equipment over and over again. Rather, you know that it's important to rotate what you use and use the weights in multiple ways.

If I were working with you online, whether it was in a face-to-face setting or in a blended learning environment, and I wanted you to learn the concept of Lifting the Weights, I'd ask you to write, speak, draw, teach, and/or explain the concept. The multiple ways will help get the concept to stick for you.

First, it's important that all teachers across your school are clear about the *it* or *its* of their lesson. Then, they can ask their students to Lift the Weights on that *it* in numerous intentional and planned-for ways throughout the session.

This intentionality will not only ensure learning sticks, but it will inform the ways a teacher or leader thinks about preparing for each session. More on that key soon!

What the Key of Engagement means for making learning stick

No matter whether it's online or face-to-face, rather than 'delivering' content, the goal is to focus on the Key of Engagement. Every learning choice teachers across your school makes involves the decision on how they will ensure that all of their students are Lifting the Weights for the majority of the time.

> **Please read this key's description out loud.**
>
> Full student engagement is essential to make learning stick. For this to happen, teachers intentionally create many opportunities for *all* students to Lift the Weights throughout the majority of the learning session.

Once embedded, your school (or schools) might use the Key of Engagement in the following ways:

What leaders do:

- Your leadership team models the Key of Engagement in all staff meetings.
- Leaders lead learning walks where the Key of Engagement is the focus of the observations.
- Instructional coaches collaborate with new teachers on ways to use the Key of Engagement.
- Lifting the Weights posters or statements are seen in the staff room, leadership offices or classrooms.
- Staff meetings take place where teachers have time to discuss how they ensure all students Lift the Weights on the *it* or *its* of lessons.

What teachers do:

- Teachers build in student movement throughout a lesson.
- Teachers think about the pacing of the lesson.
- Partners read PowerPoint items out loud to each other.
- All teachers have everyone writing first, then sharing that writing with their seating partners.
- Rather than the teacher reading a poem out loud to the class, partners read a poem out loud to each other.
- Teachers create lessons where all students are Lifting the Weights on the right *it* or *its* of the lesson.
- Students teach their notes to other students.
- A teacher knows how to use the end of the lesson in a way that makes learning stick for everyone, which means such things as writing the most important thing learned in that lesson, sharing that with another student, writing for 90 seconds a summary of the lesson, and more.

- Everyone is able to explain how they are *using* the Key of Engagement to make learning stick for everyone.

Evaluate your school's (or schools') use of this key

1. Looking at the key's description, explain which aspect of that description is your school's (or schools') strength.

2. What aspect of this key's description would help move the school from good to great?

The Key of Students

In a delivery model of education, learners are empty vessels that need to be filled. It doesn't matter who they are because information and content are 'neutral' and learners just need to learn it.

Researchers and leaders in the areas of culturally proficient teaching, critical pedagogy, multicultural education, positive psychology, literacy and education and my own doctoral work tell us that who learners are matters.

If you want learning to stick for everyone, it's important to understand that their identities (race, gender, sexual orientation, faith/religion, disabilities/abilities, languages, nationalities and so much more), strengths, interests and life experiences are integral to how learning sticks.

When teachers know who students are, they have an essential key to build a bridge between them and the content they care so much about, a tool to make learning stick.

To make this happen, it's important to remember a few things.

1. Identities always matter

If you were the only woman in a workshop full of men and every day the only text you read, stories you heard, movies you watched, or materials you studied were about men, would you be motivated to engage? In fact, what would these materials make you believe about yourself, the subject or your life choices?

If you asked all the students in that workshop if they ever thought about their gender, the men would probably say *no*; and the only female in the room, if she felt safe to share it, would probably say *yes*. The men would say *no*, not because there's something wrong with them, but because they don't have to negotiate their gender identity, while the woman does, every day.

By *negotiate* I mean:

- think about
- defend
- hide
- deny
- stand up for
- explain
- speak up for
- try to ignore

To make learning stick for everyone, this key invites teachers to remember that their students have identities and to remember that identities connect with power.

By *identities* I mean:

- race
- gender
- sexual orientation
- age
- nationalities
- religion/faith
- disabilities/abilities
- languages
- and so much more

These inform the ways in which learning sticks for everyone.

By *power* I refer not to those who have to negotiate their identities but to those who do not. Having to negotiate an identity or identities is a distraction and interferes with learning (Uehara, 2005; Lee et al., 1997; Nieto, 2000; Noordhoff & Kleinfeld, 1993).

When your team knows this, it will shape and inform the questions they ask. It also shapes the materials, images and words you use, and how teachers and leaders view the world. To make learning stick for everyone the teacher's job is to create conditions where identities are honoured, celebrated and recognised and power is shared with everyone.

2. Prior knowledge matters

You're teaching a class about farming. Some of your learners grew up on farms, helping to raise livestock and grow the crops. They spent their weekends tending the soil, helping their parents, and even managed some of the farm's finances. Meanwhile, other learners grew up in the city.

In your high school the entire school must take a class on farming. Which learners would be set up best for success?

Yep, the ones who grew up on a farm!

That's because those students have different prior knowledge of the subject than their city-living peers.

Schema theory explains that knowledge structures are acquired from past experiences and learning and from the identity and background of an individual (Moje & MuQaribu, 2003). That means learners who grew up on a farm would be set up for success in a class about farming. They would know the vocabulary and ways of being in a way that other students would not.

Teachers can't control where their learners grew up or the life experiences they've had, but they should realise that who their students are matters and build a bridge between the knowledge and the content. They can activate prior knowledge that learners might already have so that all learners can relate in some way to the content. When you understand this, you'll know how important it is to learn about your students. Only then will you know how to start your class or learning session to help all learners access the prior knowledge needed for success. It's not about who is smart or who isn't. It's often about whether or not a learner has prior knowledge. When you activate it in the right way, you're creating the conditions for learning to stick for everyone.

3. Safety matters

Have you ever been in an online group meeting where the facilitator asks the group a question and everyone goes silent, or maybe one person raises his or her hand and the rest avert their eyes and hope they aren't called on?

It doesn't necessarily mean everyone is lazy, uninterested or not wanting to participate. It means their guards are up.

Or, have you ever had a teacher who asked students to stand in a circle, then asked one person to answer a question, then asked the next person in the circle to answer the question, and so on? Everyone is nervous and thinking of their answers when their turn comes, instead of paying attention to what others are saying; and when they have shared, they are so relieved that they aren't listening to anyone else.

To help make learning stick for everyone, it's important for a teacher to consistently work to lower everyone's guard.

We call this guard the 'affective filter' (Krashen, 1982). The filter is like a drawbridge that is pulled up to keep the castle safe. When there's safety, the drawbridge goes down.

To get learning to stick, a teacher needs to create the conditions that lower their students' affective filter. When it's down, and they feel safe, they are more open to Lifting the Weights during the learning session.

When teachers across your school know their students well and have ways to consistently lower their affective filters, they are creating the conditions that ensure all students will feel safe in Lifting the Weights!

💪 Please read this key's description out loud.

Who students are matters. Students' strengths, identities and backgrounds are key to how learning sticks. For this to happen, teachers know their students well and have effective ways to link their students' lives to the content.

Once embedded, your school (or schools) might use the Key of Students in the following ways:

What leaders do:

- The librarian shares resources with teachers to help them diversify content, materials and resources so that the content connects to who students are.
- Leadership teams provide teachers with inspirational quotes or statements to prime students for learning.
- Staff meetings are held where time is set aside for everyone to discuss the Key of Students description.
- Leaders use music as the teaching team enters to lower students' guard and prime them for learning.
- Coordinating vertical teams of teachers who work together to find ways to make the lesson about the students.

What teachers do:

- All teachers meet students at the door and shake each student's hand as they enter.
- Teachers prioritise student wellbeing in service of learning.

- Everyone thinks of the identities, strengths and backgrounds of students and finds ways to build bridges between who the students are with the content.
- Teachers start each lesson by purposefully activating prior knowledge.
- Teachers start lessons by asking the kinds of questions that help all students feel connected to the content.
- Teachers set up classrooms to focus on the Key of Students.
- Teachers design PowerPoint slides that use language and images that students relate to.
- Everyone is able to explain how they are *using* the Key of Students to make learning stick for everyone.

Evaluate your school's (or schools) use of this key

1. Looking at the key's description, explain which aspect of that description is your school's (or schools') strength.

2. What aspect of this key's description would help move the school from good to great?

The Key of Classroom

In the field of early childhood education, educators understand that learning doesn't happen through *delivery* of information. Rather, learning happens through play, interaction, questions and intentional engagement. For this reason, early childhood leaders often refer to the classroom as the 'third teacher' (OWP/P Architects et al., 2014). That's because they know what it takes for learning to stick, and they coordinate the location (their indoor or outdoor environment) based on ways that help facilitate that happening.

Because your mission is to get learning to stick for everyone, you're committed to replacing *delivery* of information with creating an environment where all of your learners are Lifting the Weights. Because of this, the teacher's classroom is one of the greatest teaching strategies at their disposal. When they strategically set it up well, they're setting the conditions to make learning stick for everyone.

At its best, the classroom can help students feel safe and included, it can help surround your students with key concepts and ideas, it can prime them for learning, and it can proactively eliminate many behaviour management challenges or disruptions before they begin.

I've seen excellent teachers expand their impact through the ways they've organised their classroom, and team culture can be strengthened by the way leaders set up their meeting spaces using this key. That's because a well-set-up classroom or meeting room can do amazing things.

Years ago, a Year 7 student told me something I will always remember:

> 'I know within the first few minutes of walking into a classroom whether to take the class seriously based on how the classroom is set up.'

Here are some examples of what the classroom can do:

1. Boost learner engagement

Too often in learning situations, students are sitting passively or looking like they're engaged but instead are thinking about other things. If your schools want *all* students Lifting the Weights for the majority of the time, the classroom, if set up well, can help make this happen. In fact, it can limit the kinds of behaviour management challenges or other distractions that get in the way of making learning stick for everyone.

Remember, your teaching and learning mission is always the same: to make learning stick. With a deep understanding of this key, teachers and leaders can boost students' engagement, which you know is what makes learning stick.

By boosting student engagement, I mean reaching more students and ensuring that all of them are Lifting the Weights for the majority of the time. When your school unlocks the potential of this key, you're setting the conditions that make learning stick for everyone.

2. Prime learners for learning

Supermarket owners are intentional in the way they set up their stores. They play specific music to create a mood, set up the aisles of the store to capture your interest and at the checkout counter place specific items near you. Their intention is to entice you to buy, and they proactively prime their store for this to happen.

The internet company Amazon are intentional in the way they set up their online store. They have images, graphics, text and their checkout cart set up in ways that encourage you to buy. They use words of encouragement and even call you by your name. Their intention is to get you to buy, and they proactively prime their online space to make this happen.

A teacher's classroom can do the same thing.

When learners feel positive, safe, included and set up for success, you're proactively priming them for learning (Green, 2014; Allison et al., 2021).

3. Surround students with the content

A teacher's classroom, when set up well, can help surround students with the main ideas, topics, themes or *it* that you want them to learn.

Teachers who use this key well begin to see their classroom as a giant fish tank. The fish are their students. The water is the *it* or *its*. To help make learning stick for everyone, teachers can ensure that students swim in the *it(s)* of the content, which will help make learning happen. Soon, I'll show you how.

 **Please read this out loud:**

A well-set-up classroom creates the environment that makes learning stick. For this to happen, teachers create their own inspiring and inviting classroom, design an effective seating plan and use the classroom walls to inspire, include and teach.

Why teachers need their own classrooms

If you want to advance teaching and learning across your school, one of the most important things you can do is ensure all teachers have their own classrooms for the entire day. In fact, teachers who have their own classroom have told me:

- They're more focused.
- They're using the Unleash Learning System™ effectively.
- Their wellbeing is strengthened.
- They can set up the classroom environment in a way that consistently helps make learning stick for everyone.

- They have a sense of ownership and pride in their room.
- Behaviour management issues lessen.
- It provides them with time to plan lessons.
- They have fewer distractions.
- It's a professional game changer.

One high school teacher who has her own classroom told us that she's been offered employment at different schools but hasn't left because those schools do not provide teachers with their own classrooms.

Ensuring all teachers at your school have their own classroom is a schoolwide action that can help make learning stick for everyone (Ryan, 2020). It's putting all teachers onto their own ships so that all their time and energy are focused on sailing effectively.

How can you do this?

Scan this QR code and get instant access to our Unleash Learning TV episode on how one school was able to ensure all teachers have their own classrooms.

unleash-learning.com

Once embedded, your school (or schools) might use the Key of Classroom in the following ways:

What leaders do:

- Leaders use assigned seats in all staff meetings.
- Leaders use their office walls to surround their teaching teams with the *it* or *its* they want to stick.
- School leaders model the Key of Classroom through the set-up of the staff room.

- School leaders put inclusive images on the walls of the school (hallways, front office, office) and website, so all students feel connected to school.
- Instructional coaches work with teaching teams to put inspirational quotes or statements on the walls across the school.
- Leaders ensure that the school's website includes diverse images.
- The leadership team models the Key of Classroom in everything they do.

What teachers do:

- All teachers have their own classroom.
- Teachers intentionally set up the tables and chairs in locations that help boost student engagement.
- Teachers use assigned seats and change them to meet the needs of the learning activities.
- Teachers use the walls to surround students with the *it* or *its* of the class.
- Teachers ensure effective lighting: for example, turn on the classroom lights. (I've been in numerous classrooms where the only light is coming from the windows and the overhead projector lights with teachers telling me the students like the lights being off.)
- Teachers ensure the classroom walls are filled with diverse images and representations.
- Teachers use plants, natural light or other elements to help students feel inspired, calm or positive when in the classroom.
- Everyone is able to explain how they are *using* the Key of Classroom to make learning stick for everyone.

A NEW WAY FORWARD FOR SCHOOLS

Evaluate your school's (or schools') use of this key

1. Looking at the key's description, explain which aspect of that description is your school's (or schools') strength.

2. What aspect of this key's description would help move the school from good to great?

The Key of Inclusion

The mission of a coach of a sports team is to win the game. The coach does many things to make this happen, including ensuring team members consistently work together, successfully. The team can't win if someone is left out, one person dominates the group, or only one person is Lifting the Weights during training. In fact, many teams will take classes to learn how to work together and how to interact and communicate effectively with diverse individuals – all skills that help them work well together.

If you want to make learning stick for everyone, it's essential you think of your group of learners as one team. To do this, the Key of Inclusion is essential. Inclusion means that, as an educator, you're thinking about the group as a whole and working with your learners to create equal participation and a sense of belonging. Here's why.

1. Inclusive participation matters

As I've said, but it is worth repeating, if you want learning to stick for everyone, it's essential that all students are Lifting the Weights for the majority of the lesson. Yet sometimes we might find that the same few students raise their hand, speak during the online or face-to-face session, record their ideas and participate, while others sit and passively listen or check out.

If you want to make learning stick for everyone, it's essential to have inclusive participation of the entire group. When you're thinking about inclusive participation, you are thinking about gender, race, sexual orientation, age, language or languages, nationalities, disabilities/abilities and even the personalities of your students/participants. While related to the Key of Students, in this key we're emphasising what happens when you know your students.

The good news is: once you know the importance of this key in helping you make learning stick for everyone, there are strategies you and your learners can use together to help make this happen.

2. A sense of belonging matters

One of my favourite quotes about learners, learning and inclusion comes from Adrienne Rich (Rich, 1986), a noted poet, essayist and feminist, who said:

> *When those who have power to name and to socially construct reality choose not to see you or hear you, whether you are dark-skinned, old, disabled, female, or speak with a different accent or dialect than theirs, when someone with the authority of a teacher, say, describes the world and you are not in it, there is a moment of psychic disequilibrium, as if you looked into a mirror and saw nothing. (p. 199)*

For far too many students, learning is like looking into a mirror and seeing nothing.

But you are different. You want learning to stick for everyone, no matter whether it's online or in person. As such, it's important to know what your learners are thinking when it comes to your classroom, workshop or online location set-up, the materials you're using, activities you're creating and lessons you design:

Does this include me?	Do I belong here?	Does it relate to me?

If I'm a learner in your class and I feel like I belong, my guard goes down, my prior knowledge is activated, my experience is validated and my life is honoured. Therefore, I'm more likely to want to engage. This is what makes learning stick.

Here's something to remember. The materials you and your teaching team use, words you say, pictures you put on PowerPoint, and even guest speakers you bring to the class or workshop all send powerful messages to your learners. Without saying a word, you can ensure that, over time, everyone feels a sense of belonging.

This is especially important for communities who have been historically marginalised, silenced or excluded from our educational spaces.

 **Please read this key's description out loud.**

All students should be and feel included in order to make learning stick. For this to happen, teachers and students create an environment in which everyone sees himself/herself reflected. Learning sticks where there is inclusive participation and there is a collective sense of belonging.

Once embedded, your school (or schools) might use the Key of Inclusion in the following ways:

What leaders do:

- Leaders model ways to help create a sense of belonging.
- The librarian starts staff meetings by sharing materials that help diversify content – images, resources and other materials.
- The leadership team makes this key a focus for the semester or year.
- There is investment in schoolwide professional learning on diversity, equity and inclusion.
- Staff meetings are held where everyone discusses the Key of Inclusion description and explains how it informs their use of the key.

What teachers do:

- Teachers help students learn how to work well together.
- Teachers use inclusive language.
- Teachers share how they use the Key of Inclusion to make learning stick for everyone.
- Assigned seats are mixed up throughout the year so students get to meet and work with different students.

- Table partners shake hands at the start of a lesson and say: 'I'm so lucky to be working with you!'
- Teachers create a classroom library filled with diverse stories and people.
- New teachers work with their mentors on ways to ensure inclusive classroom participation.
- Everyone Lifts the Weights in each class and teachers find ways to pass out the weights to *all* students.
- Teachers bring in a range of guest speakers with diverse identities.
- Everyone is able to explain how they are *using* the Key of Inclusion to make learning stick for everyone.

Evaluate your school's (or schools') use of this key

1. Looking at the key's description, explain which aspect of that description is your school's (or schools') strength.

2. What aspect of this key's description would help move the school from good to great?

The Key of Plan

In the delivery model of education, educator planning isn't critical nor is the lesson design being used. In this model, teachers can decide at the last minute, even on their way to work, what they want to cover in class.

I've personally worked with more new and experienced teachers than I can count, and one thing that comes up all the time is how lesson planning is at the *bottom* of their to-do list. They have so much going on that lesson planning doesn't become a priority.

Because of this, the way your teaching team plans their lessons and the lesson plan they use are critical. The good news is: your team doesn't have to spend hours and hours planning or trying to figure out the best lesson design to use. Since your goal is to make learning stick for everyone, rather than 'teach' or 'deliver' information, there's a specific process for your lesson design that doesn't change.

Here are a few important things to know.

1. Effective planning is essential

Earlier we talked about how educators are like captains of sailing ships who know where they want to go and know that planning is essential. Sailing captains also know their ship is a system, and there are tools in the system that are essential for heading in the desired direction. That means that the captain always focuses on these tools during the planning process. A captain is effective because he or she knows what the destination is and how to ensure a safe arrival at that destination.

Without effective planning, the sailboat might get lost, get blown off course and never reach the intended location. Sailing the boat should be the fun part. This happens through effective planning.

When you embed a teaching and learning mission across your school, you're helping everyone know the intended destination for every lesson they lead. Once educators learn the tools of the system that get you to your intended destination, not only will they know that it's essential to plan effectively, but they'll consistently use that system when they plan. This will save everyone time, increase their effectiveness and help your entire school get to the desired destination. The content, group of learners or technology might change; but because everyone wants learning to stick for everyone, what they focus on during their planning process does not.

2. There are only three parts of a lesson

After nearly 25 years in the field of education, I've seen all kinds of lesson designs. Most of them are focused on teaching, not learning. Many of these lesson designs are just a tool for 'delivering information' rather than getting learning to stick. Or worse, as we discussed earlier, sometimes what sticks for students is not the content, but compliance.

But your goal is clear: you want learning to stick across your school. To do that, just know that every lesson has only three parts: a start, middle and end. And each part is critical in getting learning to stick. When your entire team understands these three parts, it will inform how they plan the lesson, create curiosity and high interest, activate prior knowledge and ensure weightlifting throughout.

I've seen behaviour management challenges disappear because of the ways classroom teachers have used the three parts of the lesson. I've spoken to instructional leaders who run full staff sessions who have told me that learning is sticking for more of their teaching team because of the ways they focus on the three parts of the lesson.

If you want to make learning stick for everyone no matter what, it is important that your school masters the three parts of the lesson. A little hint: the biggest gain to lesson designs I've seen has come from how teachers close a lesson. In fact, many teachers tell me that it's the closing that's their struggle. When everyone across your school knows how to close the lesson to make learning stick for everyone, you're helping to advance teaching and learning across your school.

3. All students need to be Lifting the Weights

At the start, middle or end of the lesson, the mission is the same – getting all students to Lift the Weights on the right *it* of the lesson. As we've discussed, you know it's essential that all students are Lifting the Weights on the *it* in multiple ways. You understand that knowing the identities of your students matters. You also know that ensuring all students are included throughout each part of the lesson is essential.

With this knowledge, teachers across your school will be focused during their planning, will be consistent in their approach and will ensure that the lessons they design and facilitate will help make learning stick for everyone.

 **Please read this key's description out loud.**

Preparation and a well-structured lesson plan lay a foundation to make learning stick. For this to happen, teachers proactively schedule their preparation time, know how to use it well and design their lessons around three distinct parts: beginning, middle and end.

Once embedded, your school (or schools) might use the Key of Plan in the following ways.

Planning

What leaders do:

- Leaders help teachers proactively schedule their preparation time and ensure it's used for lesson planning.
- Staff meetings take place where teachers have time to discuss their lesson planning process to help make it a priority across the school.

What teachers do:

- Teachers use the six keys of the Unleash Learning System™ when designing lessons.
- Teachers have their own classrooms so they have quiet spaces for lesson planning.

At the start of the lesson

What leaders do:

- Leaders model the start of lessons in staff meetings.
- Leaders provide time in staff meetings for teachers to discuss how they open their lessons based on the system.
- Leaders put posters in the staff room with examples of ways to start the lesson in order to make learning stick for everyone.
- Leaders lead learning walks where the start of the lesson is the focus of the observations.

What teachers do:

- Teachers display the lesson agenda on an overhead and have all students reading it aloud to each other.
- All teachers meet students at the classroom door and shake their hands or do an elbow bump.
- Students shake hands with their partner before they begin the lesson.

- Teachers ask all students to write first on a high-interest topic that connects to what the session is about, which activates prior knowledge.
- Students stand next to their partner, answering a series of questions with their partner regarding what they've learned in the last session.
- All students lift weights.

In the middle of the lesson

What leaders do:

- Leaders model the use of movement during staff meetings or professional learning activities.
- Leaders have all staff Lift the Weights in all staff meetings.
- Leaders invite a teacher to demonstrate the use of the middle of the lesson during a staff meeting or professional learning day.
- Instructional coaches collaborate with teachers on ways to boost student engagement in the middle of the lesson.

What teachers do:

- All students take notes during a full class discussion.
- Partners read a text out loud to each other.
- All students speak content-specific vocabulary out loud.
- Students stand or simply turn to their partner in their seat, asking their partner questions to help them check for understanding.
- Students write, speak, explain and discuss in multiple ways.
- Teachers monitor the energy of the room to ensure effective lesson pacing.
- The Key of Engagement is in full use.

At the close of the lesson

What leaders do:

- In all staff meetings, leaders have everyone write a summary explaining what the session was about, then invite table partners to share what they wrote out loud.
- The entire school considers ways to close the end of a unit, semester or school year in a way that makes learning stick for everyone.

What teachers do:

- All students write a 40-word summary of the session in their notes.
- All students explain the main concept or ideas of the session to a partner.
- All students stand in a circle reading out loud the most important part of their notes to the class.
- Table partners explain the session agenda in their own words.

Evaluate your school's (or schools') use of this key

1. Looking at the key's description, explain which aspect of that description is your school's (or schools') strength.

2. Which aspect of this key's description would help move the school from good to great?

Bringing it all together

When you make the destination *Make learning stick for everyone,* and you use the Unleash Learning System™ to get to that destination, you're helping to support a common language, limit distractions and ensure learning sticks for everyone, no matter what takes place.

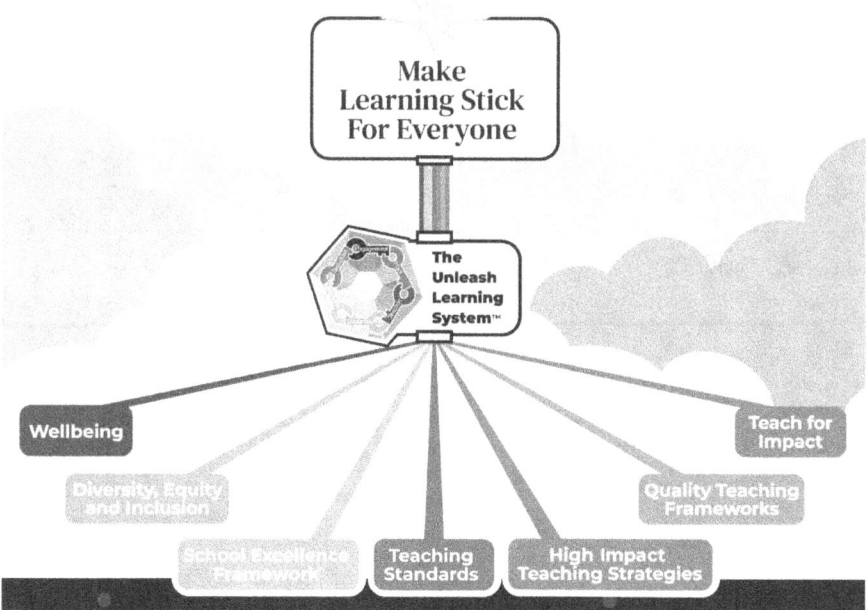

The good news is: the Unleash Learning System™ isn't *one more thing to learn* but is the system that brings everything together for you and your entire school. When new initiatives happen, you can bring those initiatives into the system, to support what's new.

This can lower stress, increase effectiveness and help your school stay focused even in the era of overwhelm.

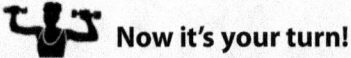 **Now it's your turn!**

Below is a list of teaching and learning initiatives. To practise how these initiatives fit within the Unleash Learning System™, take the list below and place each initiative into the key or keys you believe the initiative is connected to.

Initiative	Which key?	Initiative	Which key?
Student participation	e.g. Key of Engagement	Notetaking	
Learning intention		Lesson design	
Students with special needs		Positive climate for learning	
Lesson planning		High-impact strategies	
Student health and wellbeing		Collaborative learning	
Teacher health and wellbeing		Multilingual students	

Initiative	Which key?	Initiative	Which key?
Growth mindset		Active learning	
Multicultural education		Reading comprehension	

Systems thinking in action

 As you might recall, we discussed the impact that systems thinking can have on your entire school, especially in the era of overwhelm. That's because even when things change, your school's teaching and learning mission and system won't; and with effective implementation, over time it will become second nature for everyone to be able to explain how they're using the system to reach your school's destination of making learning stick for *all* students.

Here's an example of a systems thinking response in relation to the Key of Classroom. Please note how the keys operate together with much overlap.

Please read this out loud!

My mission is to make learning to stick for everyone. I know that it's all about Lifting the Weights (Key of Engagement), and I use the six keys in everything I do. I've designed this lesson to ensure that all my students are Lifting the Weights throughout the majority of the session. This is what makes learning stick.

To do this, my classroom is essential (Key of Classroom). In fact, it might be the most important aspect. I have assigned seats. I've been intentional with who is sitting next to whom. I know a lot about my students (Key of Students). I have a few multilingual students who might need a little extra assistance. I've seated each next to a student who I know will be supportive and encouraging. I also don't want talkative best friends sitting together because I know this will limit the ways they Lift the Weights (Key of Engagement) in the session. I also want to create a sense of belonging and ensure equal participation (Key of Inclusion). The way I have the tables and chairs arranged proactively sets this up to happen. I have students from different identities and life experiences partnered next to each other (Key of Inclusion).

One of the ways I get all my learners to Lift the Weights is through their interaction with their partner. I assign partners to sit next to each other the moment they walk into the classroom. I have them quickly get to know each other to create safety (Key of Students) and excitement and help lower the guard of all students. It only takes about three minutes of our lesson time.

My goal is to make learning stick for everyone. My seating plan is an important part of the system that helps make that happen.

But how do you embed the system across your school or schools and get to systems thinking? Great questions! It's time to explore that now.

Part 3
Advancing Teaching and Learning in the Era of Overwhelm

'Start before you're ready.'
Steven Pressfield

Chapter 6

Using a Staged Approach

You may be wondering how to implement a simple but focused teaching and learning mission, how to create a system focused on making learning stick for *all* students, how to use the system to support the wellbeing of staff and students, and how to embed the system with a laser-like focus on these goals. I want to suggest a way to move forward to create a culture that makes learning stick for *all* students, a system that will not change regardless of other demands and priorities that move through your world. The way forward, through a staged approach, supports your commitment to student success, doesn't add to the feeling of overwhelm, and creates a cohesive culture that remains stable even when so much seems to be changing.

You also may be wondering how you will know if the system is making a difference for your school and its students. Later in the chapter, I discuss how schools using the keys have collected data to monitor and inform everyone of the progress toward making learning stick for everyone, data which itself can function as a form of leadership. But more on that later. Based on years of experience and my collaboration with schools on this approach, what follows is a description of how a staged approach can work.

To begin, gather key people.

Gather key people

Depending on the size of your school, it's possible that you will want to have everyone participate in the rollout of this work. But my own experience tells me that requiring everyone to do something can create resistance. That's why the right staged approach, combined with gathering the 'key people', is essential.

The key people I'm going to invite you to gather come from three distinct communities of practice, and all of them are important for the ways you advance teaching and learning in the era of overwhelm.

1. Your success team

I call this group the success team because, together, they help lead the collective success for advancing teaching and learning through the staged approach, such as:

- leading new teacher induction
- facilitating learning walks
- modelling the system in staff meetings
- coaching teachers on the keys
- embedding the system in schoolwide documents and policies, and
- supporting systems thinking across the school, network or district.

To support transformational change, an effective success team comprises diverse members (the Key of Inclusion) and represents essential school leadership positions. A few members of the team might leave, but with this critical mass it won't stop success. Your success team includes:

- The principal
- The executive team
- Mentors of new teachers
- Department chairs
- KLA leaders
- Instructional coaches
- Aspiring leaders
- Network leaders
- District leaders
- Anyone responsible for advancing teaching and learning across your school

To get buy-in, you might ask them to read this book, attend a webinar, watch an Unleash Learning TV episode, or read an article about the era of overwhelm, or you could schedule a one-on-one meeting with each person to discuss why you'd like to invite them to join the new way forward.

Please list the people you think would be candidates for an ideal success team in the space below.

2. New teachers and their mentors

I probably don't need to tell you how tough it can be to be a new teacher. I've also seen firsthand how the era of overwhelm can make it even tougher. Yet in Australia, only half of teachers say they participated in any form of induction (Goss & Sonnemann, 2017). And in California, where I've done a lot of work, even with induction mandated by the state, many new teachers and their mentors have told me how overwhelmed they feel.

In the era of overwhelm, the Unleash Learning System™ can help lower new teacher stress, create a common language among new teachers and their mentors, and connect their induction to the schoolwide mission and system. Plus, when you create a tribe of new teachers who are learning the system together, rather than just being placed in professional learning sessions with experienced teachers, new teachers often feel empowered because they are with others going through a similar career stage.

As first-year teacher Jonathan told us, 'Before [the system], I honestly had no idea what I was doing sometimes! I was still trying to find my way around the classroom. Since starting the program last year, I've grown so much in my pedagogical practice.'

Please list below all the new teachers you currently have at your school or will have at your school.

Please list below two members of your success team who will support your new teachers with the system.

3. Experienced teachers

I want to encourage you not to require all experienced teachers across your school to join the new way forward, but to invite the key people, especially in the first few years of this process. That's because forcing all experienced teachers to engage in this work can create resistance which can undermine the process.

I've also spoken to many teachers who have shared with me that much of the professional learning they experience causes them to feel as if they aren't already doing a great job. Learning the system is about supporting experienced teachers to advance their current success and help everyone in the team be on the same page with a shared language and direction.

The key people are the experienced teachers who might be early adopters of new ideas, have a love of learning, hold positive influence across your school, or be likely to add positivity to this process.

For a medium-sized school, I've found that the right size for the first cohort is approximately 24 experienced teachers. A group of this size can help begin to create the critical mass (along with your success team and team of new teachers and mentors) needed to advance teaching and learning in the era of overwhelm. It's important that the cohort is diverse (Key of Inclusion) and spans a range of your teaching team across your school.

Please list below the 24 experienced teachers you think would be ideal candidates.

The staged approach

In the era of overwhelm, causing transformational change to happen and endure isn't always easy. Sometimes it can even fail. But with a critical mass of key people and a staged approach (AERO, 2024) to implementation, you can lessen overwhelm, keep everyone focused and give the process the time needed to create impact that lasts. The staged approach I'm going to share provides time for each cohort to learn the system, embed it and refine it for years to come. This helps support the mechanisms that make up effective professional development, which includes building knowledge, motivating staff, developing teaching technique and embedding practice (Collin & Smith, 2021, p. 3). My experience tells me this can take, at a minimum, three years of intentional and planned-for weightlifting to make change stick.

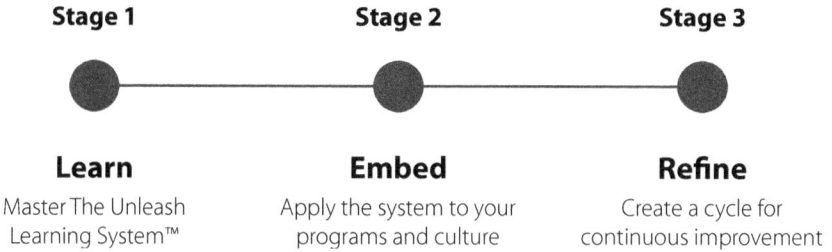

Year 1: The *Learn* Stage

In this stage each of your cohorts will learn the system and how to use it based on their role at the school. This is the year that requires the most time and effort as each key is explored in depth. Here are some of the items each cohort explores:

The success team focuses on:

- the rationale for the mission and system and keys across the school
- how to lead the Year 1 efforts, including how to support their teaching team's success and what aspects of the system to model during Year 1 activities
- a shared leadership and shared direction as a success team.

New teachers and their mentors focus on:

- the mission and system and each key in the system
- how to be successful as new teachers using the Unleash Learning System™
- preliminary actions to take to support their success using the system – including seating plan options that new teachers can use
- a shared language among new teachers and mentors at the school.

Experienced teachers focus on:

- the mission and system and an exploration of each key
- ways to use the system to optimise what they already do
- how to move away from a delivery model of education to a systems approach designed to make long-term learning stick for everyone
- determining the *it* or *its* of a lesson and how to engage all students in Lifting the Weights on it or them
- ways to build a bridge between the students and the content.

What starts to stick

In this stage it's possible you'll see change in awareness and knowledge but not practice (Ling & MacKenzie, 2001). You may see your team starting to use terms like Lifting the Weights, talking about individual keys, thinking about the *it* or *its* of their lesson, choosing individual Unleash Learning 'strategies' they want to use or beginning to update their classroom set-up based on the Key of Classroom. Yet cohorts might not see how the keys work together or how they connect with your school's teaching and learning mission.

As one teacher explained, 'The most important thing Year 1 taught me was the power of getting all my students to Lift the Weights throughout each lesson.'

Year 2: The *Embed* Stage

In this stage leaders and teachers work on embedding the mission and system across the school and in their own teaching and leadership practices. Here the teams work on actual practice, make observations, critique and engage in reflection on the use of the system (Cole, 2012). Here are some of the items your cohorts explore:

The success team focuses on:

- where to embed the system throughout the school or schools and how to support systems thinking
- how to model and use questioning to support teachers' thinking (we'll explore that soon)
- how to use data to strengthen the system (can't wait to share that!)
- how to conduct learning walks to strengthen the use of the keys.

New and experienced teachers focus on:

- how to strengthen the use of each key by determining which part of the keys represent their strength at this point and which would help them move from strength to strength
- how to engage in systems thinking with each key – that is, how the keys begin to work together
- how to refine keys through the learning walks and other observations they engage in.

What starts to stick

This is the year a shared language becomes central to the culture of the school and it becomes clear how your leadership team is facilitating the change process.

> I've seen that teachers often begin to focus on the Key of Classroom and Key of Plan but might not see the connection to the teaching and learning mission or see how all the keys connect, yet. Some leaders at this stage have reported frustration that while they see awareness across the school, they are only seeing implementation from small pockets of teachers. Yet, because of these observations, they have more information on what to focus on for Stage 3.

As campus principal Karen explains, 'Year 2 is more looking around the school, looking at what works and what doesn't work and seeing how we embed the six keys into the culture of our school.'

Year 3: The *Refine* Stage

In this stage leaders and teachers work on refining the system. Here teams discuss aspects of the keys in action, practise using systems thinking and find ways to strengthen their craft. Here are some of the items your cohorts explore:

1. Leaders learn how to evaluate the key and determine which keys should be the focus during Year 3 and beyond.
2. Leaders use metacognitive questioning to support systems thinking (see 'Using metacognition', page 116).
3. New and experienced teachers learn how to take on new information with ease.
4. To get continuous improvement, discussion groups are held throughout the year.

USING A STAGED APPROACH

What starts to stick

Systems thinking becomes more widespread across the school. More teachers and leaders start to see how the keys work together in the system. Teachers begin to use different aspects of the system and work to strengthen their craft. Everyone begins to see how the keys work together to make learning stick for everyone. And they begin to easily see where new information fits inside the system.

As one teacher at a large high school in Melbourne explained, 'By Year 3 you start to see how all the little changes become the bigger picture.'

Chapter 7

Leading the Efforts

'Be the change you want to see in the world.'
Mahatma Gandhi

Years ago I facilitated a three-month professional learning program with a group of teachers. They were committed, insightful and cared deeply about student learning. When I returned to the school a few months later, I noticed very few were using what we'd worked on. When I asked one of the lead teachers about this, she told me that no one wanted to be seen not 'doing it right', so many were waiting for someone else to go first.

I believe that statement is an important reminder about what it takes to get transformational change to happen. Some educators might feel vulnerable moving from the 'delivery' of information to working toward all students Lifting the Weights, meeting students at the classroom door as they enter, assigning seats or using the system to make learning stick for everyone.

That's why your success team is so important. Together, you'll be working to support change by embedding the mission and system inside the structure of your school or schools, supporting your teaching teams as they learn the system, and modelling the system in everything you do. These efforts will make it safe for people to take risks, try new things and reflect on their actions with others.

Embedding it into the structure

As we discussed earlier, the form creates the function. And when you embed the Unleash Learning System™ across your school, you'll help get your entire team on the same page with a shared language and direction.

To do this, I'm inviting your success team to embed the following across your school, network or district:

- the teaching and learning mission
- the system
- the key descriptions.

Questions for you (and your team):

1. Thinking about your school, network or district, where are the best locations to **embed the teaching and learning mission** to create impact and help change the culture, beliefs and behaviours?

2. Thinking about your school, network or district, where are the best locations to **embed the keys and descriptions** to create impact and help change the culture, beliefs and behaviours?

To make it stick will require you to facilitate your teams Lifting the Weights on key aspects of the Unleash Learning System™ throughout the three stages. Here are a few examples:

1. asking seating partners to read a key description out loud to each other during a staff meeting
2. placing key descriptions on the staffroom wall and asking people to write ways they use a key to make learning stick for everyone (they can write their response on a sticky note and post it on the key)
3. starting every staff meeting with everyone reading aloud your school's teaching and learning mission.

Then it's time for your team to see you modelling the system.

Modelling not mandating

Your instructional leadership activities are instrumental in supporting *all* teachers across your school to be skilled captains who can sail any ship to reach their desired destination – to make learning stick for everyone. The Unleash Learning System™ is the system they can use on any ship they sail.

If you mandate teaching strategies, it can limit critical thinking about how your teaching team sails, because they're often just complying rather than thinking deeply about how to become skilled captains sailing during times of disruption.

That's why I want to invite you to model key aspects of the system rather than mandate exactly how everyone uses the system. You can model the fact that strategies are in service of the destination and the system – they're not the destination itself.

In addition, if you and your success team model rather than mandate, you'll be helping your teaching team experience the system in action. This kind of instructional leadership supports transformational, embedded change.

A NEW WAY FORWARD FOR SCHOOLS

Want an example?

Scan this QR code and see what aspect of the Unleash Learning System™ Principal Mark Brookes models in every staff meeting.

unleash-learning.com

Using metacognition

When someone is thinking about their own thinking, we call that metacognition (Olson, 2011). Metacognition is a powerful tool that helps make learning stick for everyone, and it's a tool your success team can use to support everyone's thinking.

To use it well will require you to model an aspect of the system and then ask specific metacognitive questions.

Here's one you can use:

> How did _____ impact you as a learner?

Let's say you're modelling the Key of Engagement through having partners reading out loud to each other during the session. You can use metacognition at the end of the session to help people think about their own thinking. In this example the question would be:

> How did <u>reading out loud to your partner</u> impact you as a learner?

Then invite everyone to record their answer before picking one person in the group to respond. The key is reminding everyone that you're not asking them whether they liked doing it, but rather how it impacted them as a learner.

Then, as they respond to your question, take their response and put it back into the question. Here's an example:

Instructional leader	Teacher
How did reading out loud to your partner impact you as a learner?	It helped me pay attention to the sounds of the words.
If it helped you pay attention to the sounds of the words, how did that impact you as a learner?	By paying attention to the sounds of the words, it caused me to slow down and consider each word in the text.
If it caused you to slow down to consider each word, how did that impact you as a learner?	By slowing down, it caused me to really think about what the word means.
If it caused you to think about what each word means, how did that impact you as a learner?	It helped me make meaning of the text.
If it helped you make meaning of the text, how did that impact you as a learner?	It helped me make sure that I got what the story was actually about.

Continue the process for as long as they'll explore this with you. Usually, if you go far enough with the questioning, the person will say it's helping *make their own learning stick.*

This is the kind of modelling, combined with metacognitive questioning, that helps embed change, can create buy-in and helps teachers to think about the system.

The power of learning walks

As you probably know, learning walks are traditionally designed for leaders and educators to observe classes to strengthen student learning and create alignment across the school. But from my own experience, sometimes learning walks are not as effective as they could be, as:

- Everyone has different ideas as to what to look for.
- The school doesn't have a teaching and learning mission which informs the pedagogical approach.
- There isn't a shared common language around teaching and learning.
- People are using 'strategies or compliance' thinking, which impacts what people are looking for.
- People mistake a silent or compliant classroom with a learning classroom.

But once you've embedded your teaching and learning mission and system and have provided time for your teaching teams to start using them, learning walks will become powerful. That's because you'll have an embedded approach that contains a shared language that can support the observations. Plus, during a staged approach, I've seen teachers motivated to apply their learning because they knew other teachers and leaders would be observing their updates to their practices.

To create successful learning walks, use the Key of Plan to ensure the format is always the same:

LEADING THE EFFORTS

 Start

1. Focus on one key during the learning walk.
2. Review the key's description and provide time for everyone to **write first** about what makes learning stick for everyone based on the key's description and then **explain** their response to the partner they have been assigned to sit with.
3. Before the observations begin, ensure confidentiality is maintained so that what is seen and discussed is not shared outside of the group.

 Middle

4. Conduct the learning walk in classrooms where teachers have been embedding the system, spending less than ten minutes per classroom.
5. Invite everyone to focus on what's working well based on the key being observed.

 **End**

6. First, to debrief with the group, invite everyone to record, with a partner, what was working well based on the key being observed and then invite a few people to share their responses with the group.
7. Then, invite everyone to record the one action they'll take to strengthen their use of the key based on the observations.
8. Next, ask everyone to record how this action will help make learning stick for everyone based on the key's description.
9. To close, ask everyone to share their written response out loud with the group.

Learning walks using the Unleash Learning System™ can inspire positive change, schoolwide alignment and shared direction. They can also serve as important data for your success team to use to create continuous improvement. To explore that, it's time to talk about data.

Chapter 8

Implementation and the Use of Data

'We need to measure the things that we care about, not care about the things that are easy to measure.'

Nina Salcedo Potter, PhD

Data in the era of overwhelm

If you're working to advance teaching and learning, data offers an important tool. But I'm guessing that you and your team have more data coming to you than ever before. Even if that data provides important information, you might be finding that it is adding to your team's confusion and mental load. That's because in the era of overwhelm, more data is available with more tools for collecting it.

With the flood of data available to your school or schools, at times it can be hard to know which aspect of the data to focus on, how to translate it into teaching and learning practices that will create advancement, or how to keep up with data as it comes from outside sources that can be subject to change.

Data can also have unintended consequences. For example, data results can translate into more 'delivery' approaches to teaching and learning whereby bits of data that are seen as needing improvement are addressed through more delivery of knowledge rather than a systems thinking approach designed to make learning stick for everyone. Or as Dr Potter (DeJean, 2024) explains, 'If the data is high stakes, coming from outside sources or measuring items a school doesn't value, it can cause even more stress and disillusionment.'

In the space below, please record the data you, your team or your school are collecting or know about:

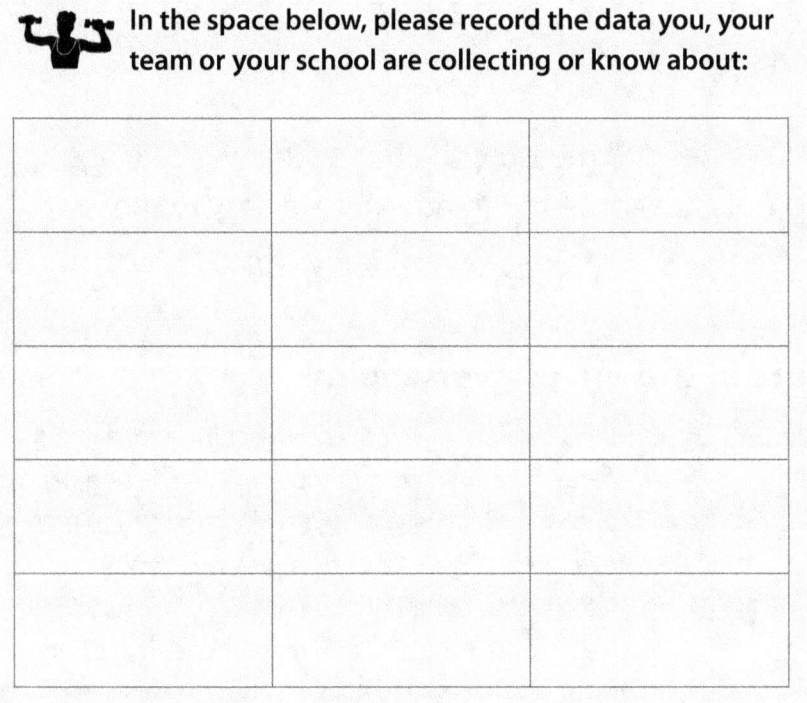

From my years of experience collaborating with teachers, leaders and schools, I have recognised two kinds of data sets that focus on teaching and learning. I call these two the **what** data and the **how** data.

The *what* data

The **what** data measures **what** your school network or state believes are important student learning outcomes. Remember the *it* or *its* we discussed earlier in the book? This data is often measuring how well these items are sticking. Some of these items come from outside sources (the state, district, network or organisation).

For example, you might have literacy measurements that track how well students are reading, writing, speaking, thinking, questioning and more; and that data examines specific aspects of items your school, network or state believe are important. This data is subject to change as new initiatives are introduced, curriculum is updated, or new expectations are raised. This data sometimes focuses on a subject area or a grade or year level, or it may be data that individual teachers want to be collected in order to measure their impact on items they believe are important.

But here we're talking about advancing teaching and learning on the schoolwide level that provides an overarching structure for other data collected. That's why you're embedding a teaching and learning mission and the system your school uses to reach it. To measure the effectiveness of this requires data focused on the **how**.

The *how* data

This data measures **how** teachers are using the craft to make learning stick for everyone. In the case of the Unleash Learning System™, this data measures how collectively the entire school is using aspects of the keys to reach its teaching and learning mission.

When you embed the system across your school or network of schools, this data source won't change even when other things do and can keep everyone on the same page with a shared language and direction.

> Reviewing the data you're currently collecting, would you say it's more focused on the **what** or the **how**?

Using data to create advancement

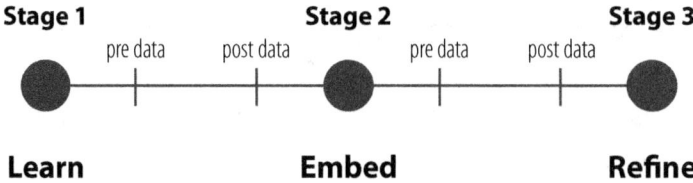

If you're working to advance teaching and learning in this era, **how** data can play an important tool as it informs progress toward the use of the system. It also provides direction toward what to emphasise as an instructional leader and how to proceed toward these objectives.

It's important to know that change takes time, so data collected early in an initiative sets a baseline from which to move forward. After a reasonable amount of time, such as toward the end of the year, with baseline data collected at the beginning, subsequent data provides feedback on progress. If the same data is collected perhaps a year later, your school can judge, over time, the effectiveness of the initiative and what adjustment or focus is needed to support the efforts.

It's also important to realise that an implementation dip might occur (Fullan, 2020) as your team begins using what might be seen as new tools and ways of thinking. But that dip can be a normal part of the process, and your success team can keep it at a minimum based on your instructional leadership activities.

The kind of data to collect

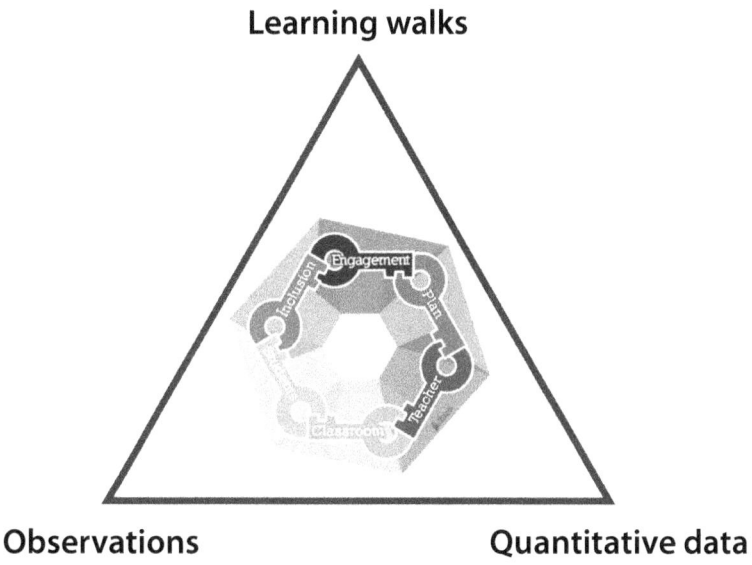

There are three points of data to consider that can help with the advancement you seek. By triangulating this data (Denzin & Lincoln, 2000) you'll have three vantage points. These vantage points can help you assess where the system is and what pieces of that system your instructional leadership can focus on to strengthen it. Over the three stages, this data can include:

Learning walks

This data comprises observations and reflections on the keys made by teachers and your success team during learning walks. For example, if the Key of Engagement is the focus of a learning walk, and observers notice that students are Lifting the Weights in class but for only small periods of time, your success team might act. For example, one campus principal in Western Australia told me that during the learning walks she noticed that engagement was taking place, but seemingly by default; so she started working to create more intentional and planned-for student engagement in all classes, something she wanted to start modelling in staff meetings.

A principal at the same school told me that during the Year 2 learning walks she noticed, much like Alex did in Melbourne (see page 54), that students were sitting most of the time. She decided she could support the strengthening of the Key of Engagement by using movement, with metacognition, in all staff meetings moving forward.

Observations

This data can be collected through your observations and those of your success team. It might involve noticing how classrooms are set up, what new and experienced teachers are talking about, or formal and informal discussions you create to discuss the keys.

For example, you might start the school year inviting staff to read the key descriptions and record which key is their individual strength and which would help them move from good to great. You might ask them to record their ideas on paper on the walls of the meeting room. These kinds of observations and discussions are important data points.

At Unleash Learning we ask success team members to conduct 'exit interviews' at the end of each year of the staged approach. Many teaching teams tell us that their learning didn't fully stick until they went through this process. That's not surprising, since the Key of Plan informs us that the closing of a lesson, unit or program, if facilitated effectively, can be the main moment of meaning-making for learners (DeJean, 2020).

These exit interviews do something else: they provide the success team with important data. For example, during the process, a success team can learn which key (or keys) are the team's strength and which key (or keys) would help them move from good to great. The success team can then decide what instructional leadership actions they can take to celebrate what's working and support ways to strengthen that key or keys.

A principal in Western Australia heard many members of his team explain how the closing of the lesson would help them strengthen their use of the Key of Plan. As a result, he began using the closing of all staff meetings to model ways to make learning stick for everyone and combined it with metacognitive questioning to help reveal everyone's thinking.

Quantitative data

This is data that can be counted numerically and can provide you with ways to assess changes over time based on specific aspects of the system.

It might be collected via a survey where teachers self-evaluate aspects of the key throughout the three-year approach or a student survey conducted anonymously.

At Unleash Learning, anonymous student surveys are completed at the start and end of the year to collect pre and post data on student experiences of learning based on aspects of the Unleash Learning System™.

A campus principal evaluated the pre-Unleash Learning data at her school and noticed that the Key of Students was a strength there. However, when she evaluated the data in more depth, she realised that while teachers do know their students well, the data showed a lower score in their ability to link content to students' lives, something she also noticed teachers talking about in their exit interview process. She decided this would be a great place to focus her efforts on to help strengthen this aspect of the key. At the end of the year, post-survey data showed a 6% increase of students who strongly agreed that this area had improved.

Using the data to create continuous improvement

'We finally have a common language!' This is what a school leader told me after the completion of the second year. At the end of that year her triangulation of data was showing her there was increased awareness of the system through what teachers were saying and what she was seeing. She told me that her instructional leadership's next steps were to support the system in becoming standard practice across the school, and from the data she knew what areas of the system to focus on that would help make that happen.

That's the power of data: it can inform you and your success team of the use of the system and where to focus on to support continuous improvement from year to year. By continuous improvement, I'm referring to the activities of observing the system and its use and knowing how to target support to strengthen its use across your school, district or network. You and your team can do this in numerous ways. Here are a few I've seen to be effective.

Evaluating pre/post data

If your school or network of schools decides to collect qualitative data around the keys, you can have your teams evaluate, together, the pre and post data. This evaluation, if done effectively and in a way that helps make learning stick for everyone, can help your teams reflect on their use of the system and determine ways to strengthen it.

Because we have a negativity bias – that is, our brains are hardwired to look for the negative, as negative emotions were designed for protection and survival (Gaffney, 2011) – the way pre and post data is shared and evaluated with your entire team is important, especially if data is showing an implementation dip (Fullan, 2020). One option is for your success team to distribute data around one key per team and invite that team to examine what's working well within that data and what they suggest the school could do to move that key from good to great. For schools using our Unleash Learning data, we offer reflective questions under each key's pre and post data for teams to use.

> In Australia it's been reported that as many as 40% of students are disengaged in any given year (Gross, 2017).
>
> Yet the post-Unleash Learning data in one school in Perth, Western Australia, indicated a boost in the Key of Engagement – a nearly 5% increase in students saying they felt engaged in class and a 7% increase in students reporting that their teachers' lessons maintained their interest.
>
> This increase took place even with teacher strike actions taking place at the school during the year.

Unleash Learning Cafés

Through the data, you're noticing that aspects of the Key of Engagement could be strengthened, and focused discussion with people using the key well can help. I refer to these discussions as Unleash Learning Cafés.

To run them, invite one 'expert' to lead a table discussion focused on an aspect of the key. These experts help your school tap into the expertise developing all around your school, rather than continuing to bring in more consultants (Schmoker, 2006). For instance, one table could focus on the use of movement while another could focus on ways to ensure students are Lifting the Weights in multiple ways throughout a lesson. These 'experts' could be members of your success team or new or experienced teachers you have observed using aspects of the keys well.

Once time is called, the expert will stay at that table and everyone else will decide which table topic they want to attend next and take detailed notes on what is being shared during each table session. Based on the time available, you might have three or four rounds taking place during the Unleash Learning Café session focused on a specific key.

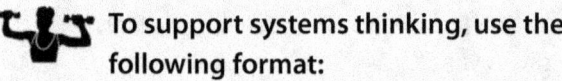 **To support systems thinking, use the following format:**

1. Based on the key about to be explored, invite everyone to record what makes learning stick based on the key description.
2. Conduct three or four café rounds, and invite everyone to take notes.
3. Invite everyone to record one action they're taking to strengthen the use of the key based on the cafés.
4. Ask everyone to record how this action will help make learning stick for everyone based on the key's description.

Focusing on the key or keys

 Data can help you create a focus. For instance, you can make a key or keys a focus of a semester, term or year. This focus will allow your entire team to explore specific aspects of the key and keep everyone focused on the areas you'd like to support for continuous improvement.

With this focus, your success team might lead professional learning days where you model aspects of this key or keys, teachers could engage in learning walks focusing on these keys, your team could facilitate Unleash Learning Cafés on this key or keys, or during a staff meeting you could have teachers who are using aspects of that key well demonstrate its use.

Instructional coaches

Instructional coaching is important work. Often that coaching is supporting individual teachers in areas in which they have decided they need support. This is fine, but if you lose that teacher, you've lost all the intellectual capital that you've invested time and resources in. Plus, that kind of individual coaching on whatever aspect the teacher wants to focus on may advance the individual, but it doesn't necessarily advance the entire school.

However, if you put a clear mission and system in place and provide instructional coaches to support the mission and system, you can support the ways all teachers are using both and directly support teachers' thinking. These are the processes that advance teaching and learning across a school.

With the Unleash Learning System™ in place, instructional coaches and teachers are having conversations about the following:

1. what makes learning stick for everyone
2. the use of an aspect or aspects of the Unleash Learning System™
3. how that use makes learning stick for everyone.

This provides a common language, a shared understanding and a common reference point to help teachers and then the school move from good to great. This also helps a teacher create a culture of continuous improvement from a systems thinking perspective.

But to create impact that endures requires a few additional steps. Before we close, let's explore them now.

Conclusion

Creating Impact That Endures

You're a leader who wants to advance teaching and learning in the era of overwhelm. You know the era is here to stay. To help your entire team stay resilient and boost their impact, you know there's a new way forward. That new way causes you to embed an ambitious teaching and learning mission – to make learning stick for everyone – across your school. This mission sets up a direction so your team can stay focused in the era of overwhelm and helps support the kind of teaching and learning that supports all students to:

- experience positive behavioural change
- experience transformative understandings
- use the important lessons, content, skills or ideas they learn
- take what they learn in every class and use it for the rest of their lives
- transcend limits.

Rather than just focusing on teaching strategies that can add to your team's overwhelm or implementing initiatives for the sake of compliance, you're embedding a simple but powerful teaching and learning system. That system can empower teachers and leaders to optimise everything they do and reduce their mental load in the process. That system provides clear definitions of great teaching and learning so you can help get to the crux of your school's thinking around high-quality teaching and learning. Also, when new information comes to your school, your entire team can quickly and easily see where this new information fits in your system.

You also know that transformational change takes time and in the era of overwhelm requires a staged approach and specific cohorts of leaders and teachers working together through those stages.

But knowing who you are, you're not satisfied with just setting this up and ensuring the system is helping empower your school to reach your collective teaching and learning mission. You want to create impact that endures. To do that, here are a few actions I invite you to consider.

1. Avoid mission creep

In the era of overwhelm it's easy for the latest new thing to throw you off course and over time cause your team to experience mission creep. Mission creep is the gradual or incremental expansion of an intervention, project or mission beyond its original scope, focus or goals, a ratchet effect spawned by initial success (Wikipedia, 2024).

Mission creep can happen when:

- the teaching and learning mission is updated or changed
- the teaching and learning mission is put on the back burner
- your team doesn't have a shared understanding of what makes learning stick for everyone
- new initiatives happen but are not used in service of the teaching and learning mission.

This can lead to:

- good captains never becoming great captains
- good schools never becoming great schools
- cynicism taking over, as the system is seen as just one more thing that comes and goes.

So, as we begin to close our time together, I want to invite you to avoid mission creep! I'm sure you'll have plenty of ideas on how to avoid it. Here are a few to consider:

1. Start every staff meeting by having everyone read out loud your school's teaching and learning mission.
2. If you use a paper agenda for meetings, ensure the teaching and learning mission is printed at the top of that agenda.
3. When new initiatives happen, provide time for the teaching teams to discuss in which key or keys the initiatives connect.
4. Avoid modifying the teaching and learning mission.

 **In the space below, explain one way you and your team will ensure there's no mission creep around the mission and system.**

2. Replace the word 'delivery'

The delivery model is so engrained in what we believe and do that even when we know there's another way, it can be tough to avoid it. In fact, even when we know what makes learning stick, we might find ourselves doing all the talking, calling on just one learner or *delivering* information throughout the lesson.

Words reflect what we think and also affect what we think. If you or your team, school or network wants to make learning stick for everyone, consider replacing the word *delivery* with a term or phrase that reflects what it takes to make that happen.

To help interrupt this old pattern, I'd like to invite you to replace the word *delivery* with something new. Here are some suggestions:

Delivery statement	Making learning stick statement
How do you deliver your content?	How do you facilitate your lesson?
How do you deliver the content?	How do you make learning stick?
We deliver our programs…	We've designed all our programs to ensure learning sticks for everyone.
This program is delivered through online learning.	The program takes place online and has been intentionally designed to make learning stick for everyone.

3. Keep focused on the key descriptions

Now you might not know this about me, but a long time ago I was a high school English teacher. And there's something I noticed that might inform your success, as it did mine.

In my class, students would read a text and then we'd have a focused class discussion. The students would debate the meaning of the text, what they thought the text was about, how it related to their lives and more.

The problem was that as the discussion took place, it was clear that they needed to go back to what the text actually said, or the discussion ended up going in all different directions. Whenever that happened, my role was to bring them back to the exact words of the text. At that point, my students would typically shift the discussion into debating what the text meant.

I share this because if you want to create impact that endures (especially in the era of overwhelm), the mission and system are essential, but so too is ensuring there's a common understanding of what each key means. This will require that your team Lifts the Weights on each of the keys often! You could do this in the following ways:

- asking everyone to write, in 30 words of less, what the Key of Engagement description means
- inviting seating partners to teach the Key of Students to each other
- providing time for everyone to read the description of the Key of Classroom then prompting everyone to draw images that represent its meaning.

To advance teaching and learning across your school, it's essential you have the mission and system embedded, a shared understanding of what each key means and time to reflect on these descriptions, often.

4. Take on new information with ease

Let's say the state is mandating that all schools roll out a new wellbeing literacy initiative. To do this, you bring an expert to conduct professional learning on the subject with your teaching team. In the era of overwhelm, even if this new information is important, you know it can flood your team with information and cause more stress. But because you have a teaching and learning mission and system, you know that wellbeing isn't your school's mission; rather it serves your mission in important ways. Or if wellbeing literacy is something the state wants all students to learn, your school knows how to use the system to integrate it and make that learning stick for everyone.

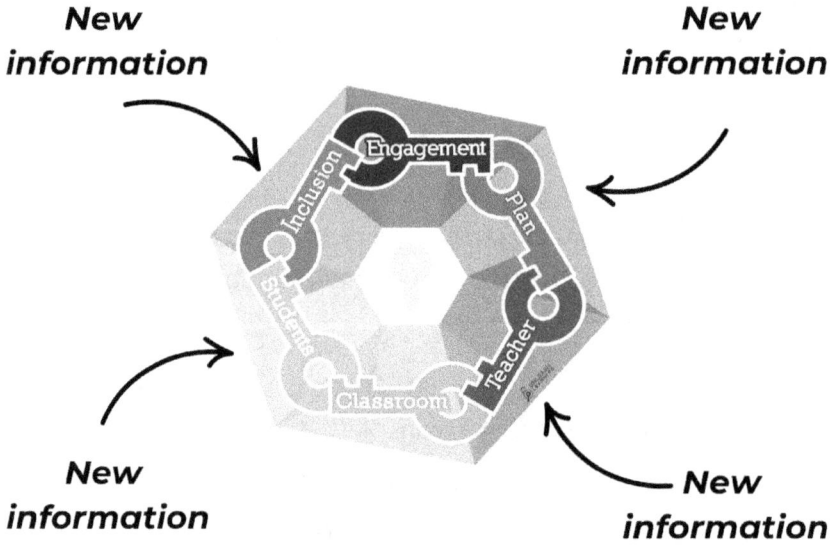

Just as importantly, with the mission and system in place you know your school can take on new information with ease. To do that, you use systems thinking during the session, helping your team see where this new information fits into your system and how it can be used to advance your teaching and learning mission.

Here's an example of how to use systems thinking to take on new information with ease.

Step 1	**Review your school's teaching and learning mission** Before your guest begins, invite everyone to read the description/s of the key or keys associated with the professional learning session about to take place.
Step 2	**Explain what makes learning stick for everyone** Next, have everyone write in their own words what makes learning stick for everyone by explaining the key's description. Then, have them read their response to their table partner.
Step 3	**Explore new information** During the professional learning session, invite everyone to take notes.
Step 4	**Act** At the end of the session, invite everyone to record the one or two actions they're considering taking, based on what they just learned.
Step 5	**Connect to the mission** To close, ask everyone to record how that action will help make learning stick for everyone based on the keys' description and share with the group.

With the mission and system in place and your school's use of systems thinking, your team can keep their mental load lowered and continue to advance teaching and learning for years to come.

Be a captain

You're doing something very powerful right now. In a culture that can feel like it's about 'keeping up' with the latest trend or teaching strategy, or if you feel like you're the tail rather than the head in all the educational changes taking place, you're taking a stand. Instead of trying to keep up with it all, you're embedding an ambitious teaching and learning mission – which is to make learning stick for everyone – and embedding a system that will help your school reach that goal.

When new initiatives come to you, and they will, you'll easily and seamlessly fit them into that system and use it to reach your destination of making learning stick for everyone. This will help you advance teaching and learning, even in the era of overwhelm.

While teachers are captains of the ship that is their classroom, you're the captain of a ship that is the entire school (or network or district). And with your success team's help, you'll be able to remind everyone of the destination and to support them in reaching it for years to come.

In the era of overwhelm, it takes courage to lead a new way forward and help everyone stay focused on it, embed systems thinking in a time of 'strategies' and 'compliance', and lead the efforts to truly advance teaching and learning across your school.

I want to invite you to be that captain and remind yourself of your courage, because after nearly 30 years in our profession, I've witnessed time and again that learning, when it sticks, can transform a student's life and help students and our world get better. Thank you for being a leader who is working to make that happen.

For good.

About the Author

I'm Dr William DeJean, founder and CEO of Unleash Learning. I'm also the host of Unleash Learning TV and Radio.

I've been deep in the education and learning field for 25 years. I have a doctorate in education and have written various article and books.

I created Unleash Learning – a new way forward for advancing teaching and learning – **because I believe in making learning stick for everyone**.

I began my career as a high school teacher in San Diego and taught for ten years across the US, winning the 2003 **San Diego County Teacher of the Year Award**.

While still teaching, I studied for a master's and doctorate in education. It was invaluable to put theories into practice and gain a broader, more inclusive understanding of how we humans learn.

I then moved into university teaching in both the US and Australia. I worked with pre-service teachers and taught teachers as they studied for their master's degrees. I developed university courses and consulted extensively with leadership teams. I gained an international perspective on education, organisational change and learning that makes a lasting impact.

In other words, I know what great learning and development looks like – and how to embed it across a team.

Whether you're inside a school or a corporate business, those same educational principles apply. It's about getting to the core of learning – so you can optimise it with an **enduring professional development system**.

I'm now based in Sydney and travel internationally to support Unleash Learning clients.

You'll also find me on the educational and professional learning circuit, presenting at public events including:

- TEDx
- Young Minds
- Happiness & Its Causes.

Next Steps

For additional information about implementing the Unleash Learning System™ and a staged approach, please use this QR code:

Or contact us directly at **unleash-learning.com**.

References

AERO. (2024). *Using a staged approach to implementation.* Australian Education Research Organisation. https://www.edresearch.edu.au/summaries-explainers/explainers/using-staged-approach-implementation

Allison, L., Waters, L., & Kern, M. L. (2021). Flourishing classrooms: Applying a systems-informed approach to positive education. *Contemporary School Psychology*, 25, 396–405.

Brookfield, S. D. (2017). *Becoming a critically reflective teacher.* John Wiley & Sons.

Cole, P. (2012). *Linking effective professional learning with effective teaching practice.* Australian Institute for Teaching and School Leadership.

Collin, J., & Smith, E. (2021). *Effective professional development: Guidance report.* Education Endowment Foundation.

DeJean, W. (2015). *Unleash learning: 40 successful strategies to ignite, inspire and unleash learning for everyone* (Australian ed.). ARMEDIA.

DeJean, W. (2020). *Make learning stick for everyone: Learn the system for online, face-to-face and blended learning environments.* ARMEDIA.

DeJean, W. (Host) (2024, March 5). Data: Here's how to use it to move good teaching to great teaching across your school. *Unleash Learning TV.* [Video]. YouTube. https://www.youtube.com/watch?v=mLof1DVhkZQ

Denzin, N. K., & Lincoln, Y. S. (2000). *Handbook of qualitative research* (2nd ed.). SAGE Publications.

Falecki, D. (2023). *Thrive: Practical strategies to nourish teacher wellbeing.* Amba Press.

Ford, D. (1999). *The dark side of the light chasers: Reclaiming your power, creativity, brilliance, and dreams.* Riverhead Books.

Fredrickson, B. (2009). *Positivity.* Crown Publishers.

Freire, P. (1975). *Pedagogy of the oppressed.* Penguin Education.

Fullan, M. (2020). Leading in a culture of change (2nd ed.). Wiley.

Gaffney, M. (2011). *Flourishing: How to achieve a deeper sense of well-being, meaning, and purpose – even when facing adversity.* Penguin Books.

Goss, P., & Sonnemann, J. (2017). *Engaging students: Creating classrooms that improve learning.* Grattan Institute.

Green, S. (2014). *Positive education: An Australian perspective*. Routledge.
Greene, M. (1988). *The dialectic of freedom*. Teachers College Press.
Hooks, B. (2001). *All about love: New visions* (1st Perennial ed.). Perennial.
Krashen, S. D. (1982). *Principles and practice in second language acquisition*. Elsevier Science & Technology.
Lakoff, G., & Johnson, M. (2008). *Metaphors we live by*. University of Chicago Press.
Lee, E., Menkart, D., & Okazawa-Rey, M. (1997). *Beyond heroes and holidays: A practical guide to K–12 anti-racist, multicultural education and staff development*. Teaching for Change.
Ling, L. M., & MacKenzie, N. (2001). The professional development of teachers in Australia. *European Journal of Teacher Education, 24*(2), 87–98.
Marzano, R. J. (2007). *The art and science of teaching: A comprehensive framework for effective instruction*. Association for Supervision and Curriculum Development.
Moje, E. B., & MuQaribu, M. (2003). Literacy and sexual identity. *Journal of Adolescent & Adult Literacy, 47*(3), 204–8.
Neisser, U. (1967). *Cognitive psychology*. Psychology Press.
Nieto, S. (2000). *Affirming diversity: The sociopolitical context of multicultural education* (3rd ed.). Longman.
Noordhoff, K., & Kleinfeld, J. (1993). Preparing teachers for multicultural classrooms. *Teaching and Teacher Education, 9*(1), 27–39.
Olson, C. B. (2011). *The reading/writing connection: Strategies for teaching and learning in the secondary classroom*. Pearson.
OWP/P Architects, VS Furniture, & Bruce Mau Design. (2014). *The third teacher: 79 ways you can use design to transform teaching & learning*. Abrams.
Palmer, P. J. (1998). *The courage to teach: Exploring the inner landscape of a teacher's life*. Jossey-Bass.
Plass, J. L., Moreno, R., & Brünken, R. (2010). *Cognitive load theory*. Cambridge University Press.
Pressfield, S. (2014). *Do the work! Overcome resistance and get out of your own way*. Black Irish Books.
Rich, A. (1986). *Blood, bread, and poetry: Selected prose*, 1979–1985. Norton.
Ryan, M. (2020). A classroom of my own. *LeadershipEd*, (10), 30–35.
Schmoker, M. (2006). *Results now: How we can achieve unprecedented improvements in teaching and learning*. ASCD.
Seligman, M. E. P. (2011). *Flourish: A visionary new understanding of happiness and well-being*. Atria Books.
Uehara, D. L. (2005). Diversity in the classroom: Implications for school counselors. *Multicultural Perspectives, 7*(4), 46–53.
Wheatley, M. J. (2017). *Who do we choose to be: Facing reality, claiming leadership, restoring sanity*. Berret-Koehler.
Wheatley, M. J. (2024). *Restoring sanity: Practices to awaken generosity, creativity, and kindness in ourselves and our organisations*. Berrett-Koehler.
Wikipedia (2024, Jan 19). Mission Creep. In *Wikipedia*. https://en.wikipedia.org/wiki/Mission_creep
Wink, J. (2000). *Critical pedagogy: Notes from the real world*. Longman.

www.ingramcontent.com/pod-product-compliance
Lightning Source LLC
Chambersburg PA
CBHW052048070526
44584CB00017B/2093